INTRODUCING

MATH! GRADE 2

ARGOPREP

AF864992

FREE VIDEO EXPLANATIONS

600 QUESTIONS TO PRACTICE

TEACHER RECOMMENDED

TOPICS COVERED

PRACTICE MAKES PERFECT

- Operations & Algebraic Thinking
- Numbers and Operation in Base Ten
- Measurement and Data
- Geometry

ArgoPrep is one of the leading providers of supplemental educational products and services. We offer affordable and effective test prep solutions to educators, parents and students. Learning should be fun and easy! For that reason, most of our workbooks come with detailed video answer explanations taught by one of our fabulous instructors.

Our goal is to make your life easier, so let us know how we can help you by e-mailing us at: info@argoprep.com.

ARGOPREP

ALL RIGHTS RESERVED
Copyright © 2020 by Argo Prep, Inc.

ISBN: 978-1946755759
Published by Argo Brothers, Inc.

All rights reserved, no part of this book may be reproduced or distributed in any form or by any means without the written permission of Argo Brothers, Inc. All the materials within are the exclusive property of Argo Brothers, Inc.

Aknowlegments:
Icons made by Freepik, Creaticca Creative Agency, Pixel perfect , Pixel Buddha, Smashicons, Twitter , Good Ware, Smalllikeart, Nikita Golubev, monkik, DinosoftLabs, Icon Pond from www.flaticon.com

- ArgoPrep is a recipient of the prestigious **Mom's Choice Award**.
- ArgoPrep also received the 2019 **Seal of Approval** from Homeschool.com for our award-winning workbooks.
- ArgoPrep was awarded the 2019 **National Parenting Products Award, Gold Medal Parent's Choice Award** and **the Tillywig Brain Child Award.**

Want an amazing offer from ArgoPrep?

7 DAY ACCESS

to our online premium content at **www.argoprep.com**

Online premium content includes practice quizzes and drills with video explanations and an automatic grading system.

Chat with us live at **www.argoprep.com** for this exclusive offer.

ARGOPREP

TABLE OF CONTENTS

Chapter 1 - Operations and Algebraic Thinking **10**

1.1. Represent and solve word problems 12

1.2. Add and subtract within 20 25

1.3. Understand Even and Odd Numbers 35

1.4. Chapter Test 49

Chapter 2 - Numbers & Operation in Base Ten **56**

2.1. Understanding Three Digit Numbers 58

2.2. Adding and Subtracting 81

2.3. Chapter Test 111

Chapter 3 - Measurement & Data **118**

3.1. Using Tools to Measure 120

3.2. Using Addition and Subtraction to Solve Word Problems 147

3.3. Working with Time and Money 162

3.4. Represent Data 176

3.5. Chapter Test 192

Chapter 4 - Geometry **198**

4.1. Recognizing and Drawing Shapes 200

4.2. Chapter Test 219

Chapter 5 - Mixed Assessment **226**

Answer Key **256**

HOW TO USE THE BOOK

Welcome to the **Introducing Math!** series by ArgoPrep.
This workbook is designed to provide you with a comprehensive overview of Grade 2 mathematics.

While working through this workbook, be sure to read the topic overview that will give you a general foundation of the concept. At the end of each chapter, there is a chapter test that will assess how well you understood the topics presented.

This workbook comes with free digital video explanations that you can access on our website. If you are unsure on how to answer a question, we strongly recommend watching the video explanations, as they will reinforce the fundamental concepts.

We strive to provide you with an amazing learning experience. If you have any suggestions or need further assistance, don't hesitate to email us at info@argoprep.com or chat with us live on our website at www.argoprep.com

HOW TO WATCH VIDEO EXPLANATIONS

IT IS ABSOLUTELY FREE

Download our app:
ArgoPrep Video Explanations
to access videos on any mobile device or tablet.

or

Step 1 - Visit our website at: www.argoprep.com/k8
Step 2 - Click on the Video Explanations button located on the top right corner.
Step 3 - Choose the workbook you have and enjoy video explanations.

OTHER BOOKS BY ARGOPREP

Here are some other test prep workbooks by ArgoPrep you may be interested in. All of our workbooks come equipped with detailed video explanations to make your learning experience a breeze! Visit us at **www.argoprep.com**

COMMON CORE MATH SERIES

COMMON CORE ELA SERIES

INTRODUCING MATH!

Introducing Math! by ArgoPrep is an award-winning series created by certified teachers to provide students with high-quality practice problems. Our workbooks include topic overviews with instruction, practice questions, answer explanations along with digital access to video explanations. Practice in confidence - with ArgoPrep!

SCIENCE SERIES

Science Daily Practice Workbook by ArgoPrep is an award-winning series created by certified science teachers to help build mastery of foundational science skills. Our workbooks explore science topics in depth with ArgoPrep s 5 E S to build science mastery.

KIDS SUMMER ACADEMY SERIES

ArgoPrep's **Kids Summer Academy** series helps prevent summer learning loss and gets students ready for their new school year by reinforcing core foundations in math, english and science. Our workbooks also introduce new concepts so students can get a head start and be on top of their game for the new school year!

SUMMER ACTIVITY PLAYGROUND SERIES

Summer Activity Playground is another summer series that is designed to prevent summer learning loss and prepares students for the new school year. Students will be able to practice math, ELA, science, social studies and more! This is a new released series that offers the latest aligned learning standards for each grade.

FrogYogi Math Series

It combines fun and engaging activities along with math concepts. Your child will be hooked in learning math on a daily basis. This workbook includes fun and effective yoga math breaks between solving problems helping the brain relax and retain more information.

Chapter 1:

Operations & Algebraic Thinking

1.1 Represent and Solve Word Problems page 12

1.2 Add and Subtract within 20 page 25

1.3 Work with Equal Groups page 35

1.4 Chapter Test page 49

ARGOPREP

ARGOPREP

1.1. Represent and Solve Word Problems

We can use equations and drawings to help us solve word problems. Let's look at an example.

There are 34 students at camp. 15 students leave camp at lunch time.
How many students are left after lunch?

Writing an Equation

Writing an equation can help you better understand what the problem is asking you to do.

There are 34 students at camp. 15 students leave camp at lunch time. How many students are left after lunch?

We can see that we start with 34 students. We can also see that 15 students leave, which signals subtraction. So, our equation is...

$$34 - 15 = \_\_\_$$

Using a Drawing

A drawing can help us solve word problems. Since this word problem uses larger numbers, we can use a number line instead of drawing each person.

There are 34 students at camp. 15 students leave camp at lunch time. How many students are left after lunch?

We know to mark the end of our number line at 34 because that's how many students we have at the beginning of the problem. We need to hop backward on the number line 15 times since it's a subtraction problem.

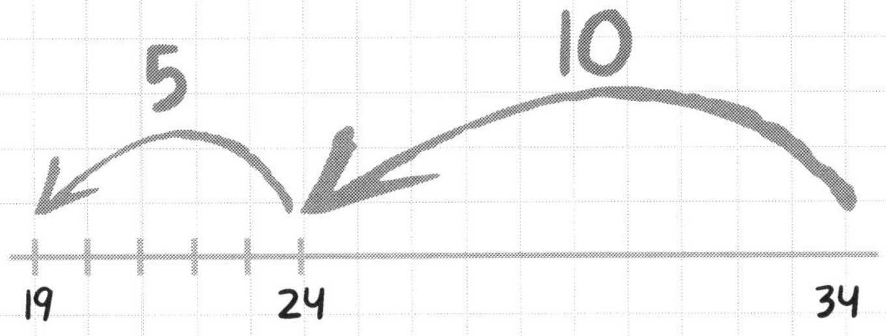

We can quickly hop back ten.

Then we need to hop back **5** more.

$34 - 15 = 19$ ✓

Let's try again with a more complicated word problem.

Sarah has 45 cookies. Her brother eats 7 of the cookies. Then her friend brings her 9 cookies. How many cookies does Sarah have after her friend brings her more cookies?

Equations

This is a two-step problem. That means there is more than one operation.

Sarah has 45 cookies. Her brother eats 7 of the cookies. Then her friend brings her 9 cookies.

The equation is $45 - 7 + 5 = \_\_\_$

Using a Drawing

Since this word problem uses larger numbers, we can use a number line instead of drawing each cookie.

We know to start at 45 because that's how many cookies we have at the beginning of the problem. We need to hop backwards on the number line 7 times since the first step is subtraction. Then we need to hop forward 5 times since the second step is addition.

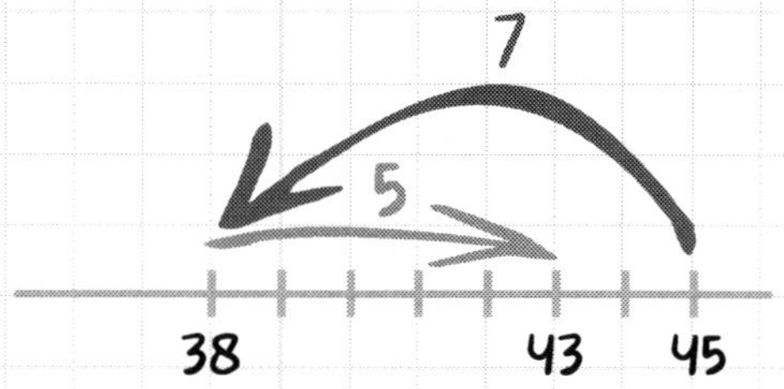

First hop back 7

Then hop forward 5

$$45 - 7 + 5 = 43$$ ✓

NOTES

Practice Questions

1. There are 17 ducks swimming in a pond. 13 more ducks waddle into the pond. How many ducks are in the pond? Represent the problem with an equation or drawing.

SHOW YOUR WORK

2. The baker made **25** cookies. The kids ate some of the cookies. There were **5** cookies left when the kids left. How many cookies did the kids eat? Represent the problem with an equation or drawing.

SHOW YOUR WORK

3. The gardener planted several pink flowers in the morning. She planted **46** more pink flowers in the afternoon. There were **60** total pink flowers when she finished. How many pink flowers did the gardener plant that morning? Represent the problem with an equation or drawing.

SHOW YOUR WORK

4. 36 big dogs and 27 small dogs are in the park. How many dogs are in the park? Represent the problem with an equation or drawing.

SHOW YOUR WORK

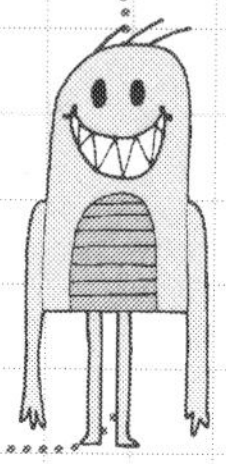

5. There are 12 cupcakes in the box. 4 are vanilla. The rest are chocolate. How many cupcakes are chocolate? Represent the problem with an equation or drawing.

SHOW YOUR WORK

6. John had 13 pieces of candy. Jane has 15 pieces of candy. How many more pieces of candy does Jane have than John? Represent the problem with an equation or drawing.

SHOW YOUR WORK

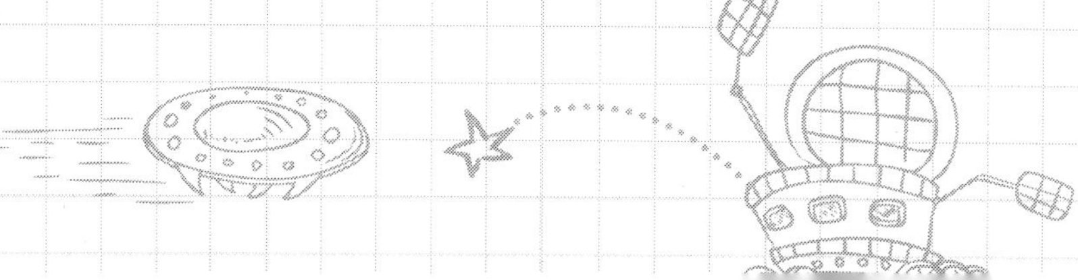

7. Sloane has 17 pencils. Nolan has 21 pencils. How many fewer pencils does Sloane have than Nolan? Represent the problem with an equation or drawing.

SHOW YOUR WORK

8. There are **51** apples in a tree. **30** apples fall off. How many apples are left in the tree? Represent the problem with an equation or drawing.

SHOW YOUR WORK

9. The baker puts **63** blueberries and 17 strawberries in the pie. How many berries are in the pie? Represent the problem with an equation or drawing.

SHOW YOUR WORK

10. There are **35** pumpkins in the pumpkin patch before the kids arrive. The kids buy many of the pumpkins. There are **3** pumpkins left after the kids leave. How many pumpkins did the kids buy? Represent the problem with an equation or drawing.

SHOW YOUR WORK

11. Sarah picked red and green apples. She picked **56** green apples and **43** red apples. How many apples did she pick in all? Represent the problem with an equation or drawing.

SHOW YOUR WORK

12. The grey kitten and black kitten weigh **21** pounds all together. The grey kitten is **9** pounds. How much does the black kitten weigh? Represent the problem with an equation or drawing.

SHOW YOUR WORK

13. A sea turtle laid 98 eggs in her nest. 74 of the eggs hatched. How many eggs have not hatched? Represent the problem with an equation or drawing.

SHOW YOUR WORK

14. Lauren's family drives 86 miles to the soccer tournament. Baylee's family drives 65 miles to the tournament. How many more miles did Lauren's family drive than Baylee's family? Represent the problem with an equation or drawing.

SHOW YOUR WORK

15. Kyle's garden has 32 more flowers than Brandon's garden. Brandon's garden has 23 flowers. How many flowers are in Kyle's garden? Represent the problem with an equation or drawing.

SHOW YOUR WORK

16. William bakes **24** cookies. His brother eats **8** of the cookies. Then William bakes **6** more cookies. How many cookies does William have now? Represent the problem with an equation or drawing.

SHOW YOUR WORK

17. Frank's mom gives him a plate with **82** peas. He quickly eats **5** of the peas. Then his mom puts **8** more peas on his plate. How many peas are on Frank's plate now? Represent the problem with an equation or drawing.

SHOW YOUR WORK

18. John's mom fills **39** water balloons. John and his brother pop **9** of the balloons. Then their mom fills up **3** more water balloons. How many water balloons do they have now? Represent the problem with an equation or drawing.

SHOW YOUR WORK

19. There are **85** students in first grade at the beginning of the year. **2** students move away. Then **5** new students join the grade. How many students are now in first grade? Represent the problem with an equation or drawing.

SHOW YOUR WORK

20. There are **12** kids at camp. **3** kids leave camp before lunch. A few more kids leave after lunch. There are now **6** kids left at camp. How many kids left camp after lunch? Represent the problem with an equation or drawing.

SHOW YOUR WORK

21. Georgia collects **54** seashells. She gives **5** to her brother and **4** to her sister. How many seashells does she have left in her collection? Represent the problem with an equation or drawing.

SHOW YOUR WORK

22. Patrick has 93 books. Thea has 14 fewer books than Patrick. How many books does Thea own?

SHOW YOUR WORK

23. Sarah has 23 fewer dollars than Steven. Sarah has 34 dollars. How many dollars does Steven have?

SHOW YOUR WORK

24. Daniel mows 32 more lawns than Jane. Jane mows 13 lawns. How many lawns does Daniel mow?

SHOW YOUR WORK

25. Zane has 23 cups for the party. 2 are blue and 3 are green. The rest are black. How many of the cups are black?

SHOW YOUR WORK

26. There are 63 students at the playground. Some more students show up after lunch. Now there are 90 students at the playground. How many students showed up after lunch?

SHOW YOUR WORK

27. There are some birds in a tree. 23 are blue birds 17 are robins.
How many birds are in the tree?

SHOW YOUR WORK

28. There are **35** cookies at the party. The guests eat **9** cookies before dinner. They eat **6** cookies after dinner. How many cookies are left after the party?

SHOW YOUR WORK

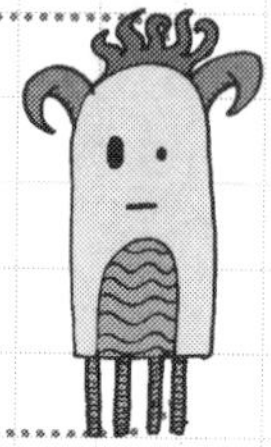

29. There are **96** students at the school. **48** of the students have blue eyes. The rest of the students do not have blue eyes. How many students do not have blue eyes?

SHOW YOUR WORK

30. The grey squirrel collects **15** more nuts than the red squirrel. The grey squirrel collects **67** nuts. How many nuts does the red squirrel collect?

SHOW YOUR WORK

Add and Subtract within 20

We can use a variety of mental strategies to solve addition and subtraction problems.

Addition

Counting On	Decomposing Numbers
9 + 2 = Start at the larger number and count on. 9 ... 10 ... 11	9 + 2 = We know that 9 and 1 is 10 We can break 2 into 1 and 1. 10 + 1 = 11

Subtraction

Using Number Relationships	Creating an Easier Problem
16 - 9 = We know that 9 plus 7 equals 16 So, 16 - 9 must be 7	16 - 9 = Instead of 16 - 9, we can add 1 to each of the numbers to make the problem 17 - 10. We can see that the answer to that problem is 7. So, 16 - 9 = 7 too

Practice Questions

1. 17 + 3 = ___ Explain your strategy.

SHOW YOUR WORK

2. 13 + 9 = ___ Explain your strategy.

SHOW YOUR WORK

3. 8 + 29 = ___ Explain your strategy.

SHOW YOUR WORK

4. 4 + 13 = ___ Explain your strategy.

SHOW YOUR WORK

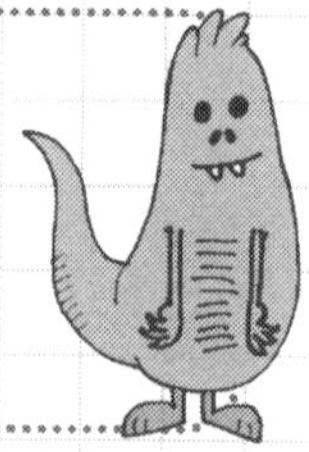

5. 8 + 6 = ___ Explain your strategy.

SHOW YOUR WORK

6. 9 + 5 = ___ Explain your strategy.

SHOW YOUR WORK

7. 18 + 2 = ___ Explain your strategy.

SHOW YOUR WORK

8. 15 + 3 = ___ Explain your strategy.

SHOW YOUR WORK

9. 11 + 5 = ___ Explain your strategy.

SHOW YOUR WORK

10. 13 + 7 = ___ Explain your strategy.

SHOW YOUR WORK

11. 20 - 7 = ___ Explain your strategy.

SHOW YOUR WORK

12. 13 - 6 = ___ Explain your strategy.

SHOW YOUR WORK

13. 14 - 5 = ___ Explain your strategy.

SHOW YOUR WORK

14. 17 - 12 = ___ Explain your strategy.

SHOW YOUR WORK

15. 19 - 8 = ___ Explain your strategy.

SHOW YOUR WORK

16. 11 - 9 = ___ Explain your strategy.

SHOW YOUR WORK

17. 12 - 5 = ___ Explain your strategy.

SHOW YOUR WORK

18. 8 - 6 = ___ Explain your strategy.

SHOW YOUR WORK

19. 18 - 6 = ___ Explain your strategy.

SHOW YOUR WORK

20. 19 - 12 = ___ Explain your strategy.

SHOW YOUR WORK

21. Fill in the missing number for the equation below. Explain your strategy.

$10 - \_\_\_ = 5$

SHOW YOUR WORK

22. Fill in the missing number for the equation below. Explain your strategy.

$3 + \_\_\_ = 17$

SHOW YOUR WORK

23. Fill in the missing number for the equation below. Explain your strategy.

$5 + \_\_\_ = 19$

SHOW YOUR WORK

24. Fill in the missing number for the equation below. Explain your strategy.

12 + ___ = 20

SHOW YOUR WORK

25. Fill in the missing number for the equation below. Explain your strategy.

6 + ___ = 19

SHOW YOUR WORK

26. Fill in the missing number for the equation below. Explain your strategy.

20 - ___ = 15

SHOW YOUR WORK

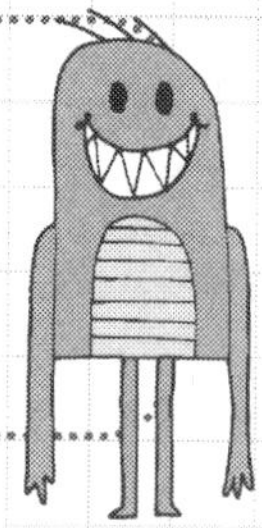

27. Fill in the missing number for the equation below. Explain your strategy.

11 - ___ = 3

SHOW YOUR WORK

28. Fill in the missing number for the equation below. Explain your strategy.

17 - ___ = 13

SHOW YOUR WORK

29. Fill in the missing number for the equation below. Explain your strategy.

14 - ___ = 9

SHOW YOUR WORK

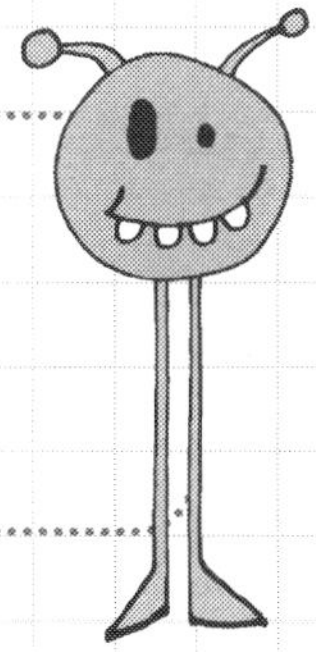

30. Fill in the missing number for the equation below. Explain your strategy.

19 - ___ = 13

SHOW YOUR WORK

NOTES

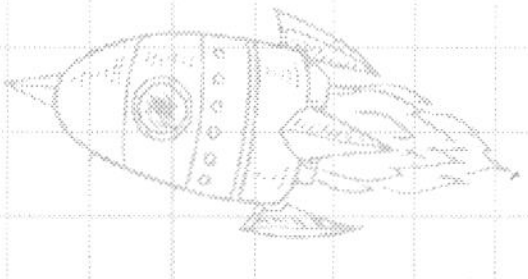

1.3.A | Understanding Even and Odd Numbers

In second grade, we need to be able to determine if a number is even or odd. An even number is a number that is made of two equal parts with no leftovers. An odd number is a number that cannot be made of two equal parts - it always has leftovers.

How can I tell if a number is even or odd?

Pairing

Is the number 5 even?

We can represent the number 5 with a drawing. If we draw 5 circles, we can see that we will have 2 pairs with one leftover. That means 5 is not even. It's odd.

Grouping

Is the number 8 even?

We can represent the number 8 with a drawing. If we draw 8 circles, we can split the circles into two equal groups without any leftovers. That means 8 is an even number.

1.3.A Understanding Even and Odd Numbers

Practice Questions

1. Is there an even number of strawberries below? Justify your thinking.

SHOW YOUR WORK

2. Is there an even number of hot dogs below? Justify your thinking.

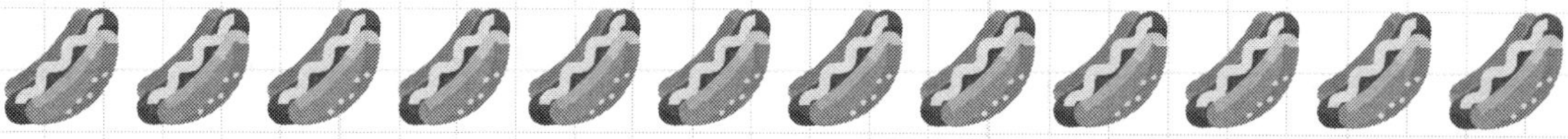

SHOW YOUR WORK

3. Is there an even number of bananas below? Justify your thinking.

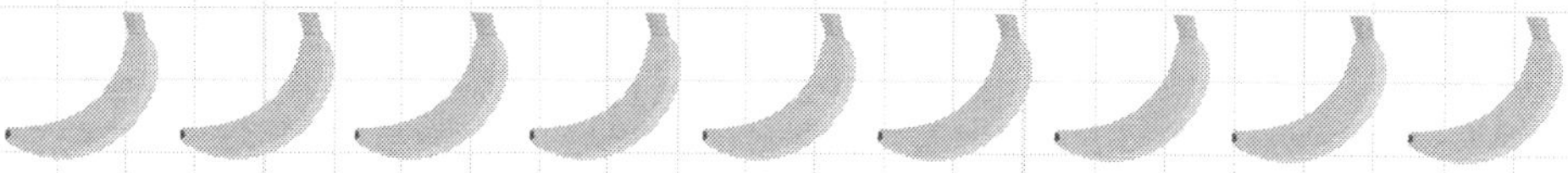

SHOW YOUR WORK

1.3.A Understanding Even and Odd Numbers

4. Write an equation to represent the number of apples below. Is the number even or odd?

SHOW YOUR WORK

5. Write an equation to represent the number of carrots below. Is the number even or odd?

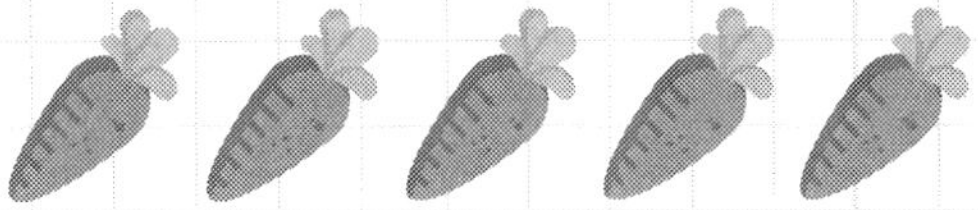

SHOW YOUR WORK

6. Write an equation to represent the number of fish below. Is the number even or odd?

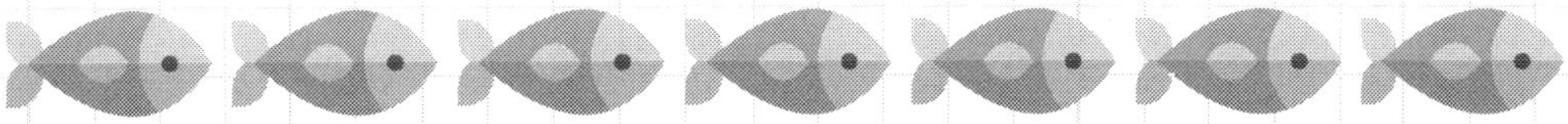

SHOW YOUR WORK

1.3.A Understanding Even and Odd Numbers

7. Write an equation to represent the number of pineapples below. Is the number even or odd?

SHOW YOUR WORK

8. Write an equation to represent the number of cupcakes below. Is the number even or odd?

SHOW YOUR WORK

9. Is 16 an even number? Justify your thinking.

SHOW YOUR WORK

10. Is 7 an even number? Justify your thinking.

SHOW YOUR WORK

11. Is 15 an even number? Justify your thinking.

SHOW YOUR WORK

12. Is 18 an even number? Justify your thinking.

SHOW YOUR WORK

13. Is 12 an even number? Justify your thinking.

SHOW YOUR WORK

14. Is 19 an even number? Justify your thinking.

SHOW YOUR WORK

15. Is 13 an even number? Justify your thinking.

SHOW YOUR WORK

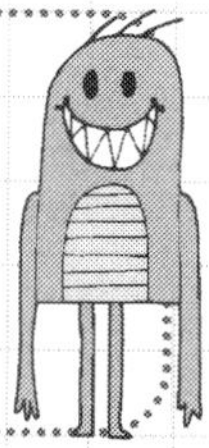

NOTES

Adding Equal Groups

We can use repeated addition to quickly count a large group of objects. Let's give it a try!

What is the total number of stars below? Justify your thinking using repeated addition.

Step 1: Determine the number of stars in each row

We can see that there are 4 stars in each row

Step 2: Determine the number of rows

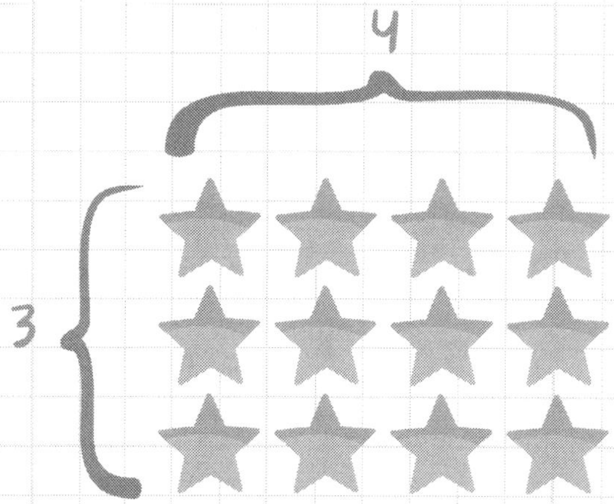

We can see that there are 3 rows

Step 3: Write an equation

4 + 4 + 4 = ___

There are 3 groups of 4

Step 5: Solve

4 + 4 + 4 = 12 ✓

NOTES

1.3.B Understanding Even and Odd Numbers

Practice Questions

1. What is the total number of hearts below? Justify your thinking using repeated addition.

SHOW YOUR WORK

2. What is the total number of stars below? Justify your thinking using repeated addition.

SHOW YOUR WORK

3. What is the total number of diamonds below? Justify your thinking using repeated addition.

SHOW YOUR WORK

4. What is the total number of suns below? Justify your thinking using repeated addition.

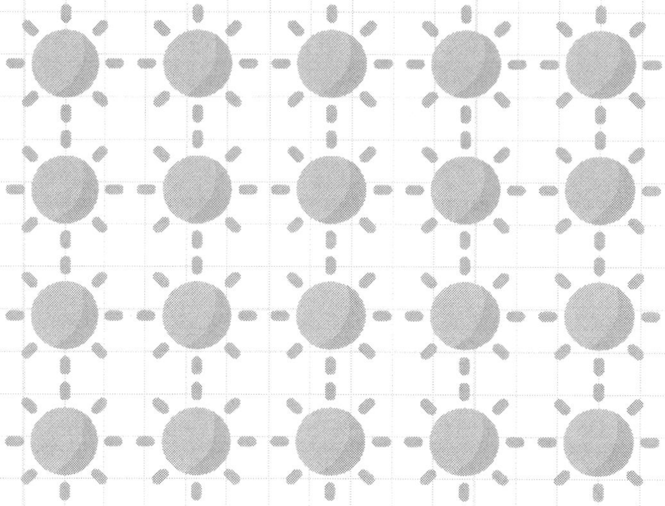

SHOW YOUR WORK

5. What is the total number of rainbows below? Justify your thinking using repeated addition.

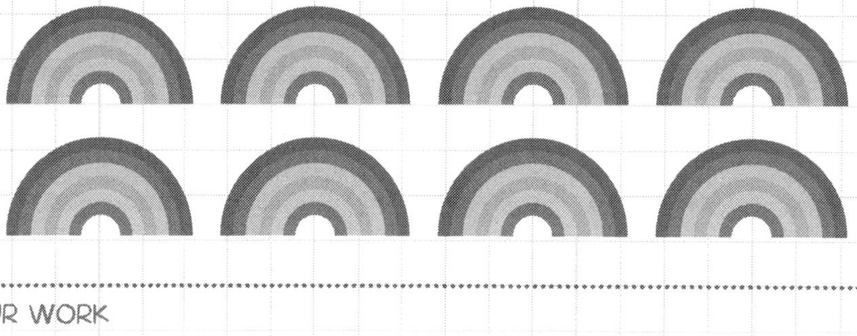

SHOW YOUR WORK

6. Write an equation to represent the total number of hearts below.

SHOW YOUR WORK

7. Write an equation to represent the total number of stars below.

SHOW YOUR WORK

8. Write an equation to represent the total number of diamonds below.

SHOW YOUR WORK

9. Write an equation to represent the total number of suns below.

SHOW YOUR WORK

10. Write an equation to represent the total number of rainbows below.

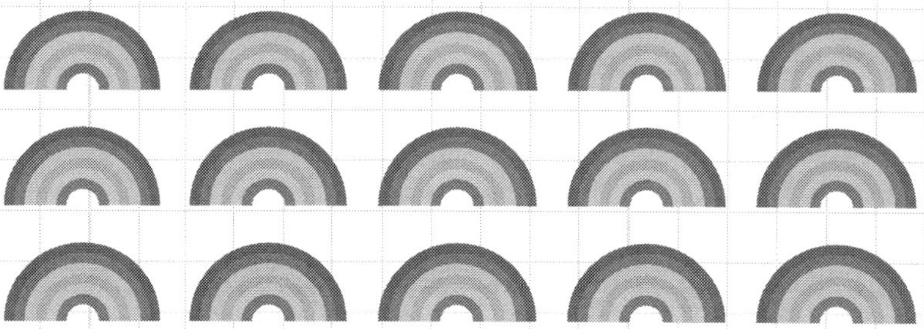

SHOW YOUR WORK

11. Chris draws 5 rows of circles. Each row contains two circles. How many circles did he draw?

SHOW YOUR WORK

12. Sarah fills a box with blocks. She fills the box with 4 rows of blocks and 3 blocks in each row. How many blocks are in the box?

SHOW YOUR WORK

13. John uses tiles to make a rectangle. He makes 3 rows of tiles and 2 columns of tiles. How many tiles did he use?

SHOW YOUR WORK

14. Draw a rectangle with two rows of circles and two columns of circles. How many circles are there in your rectangle?

SHOW YOUR WORK

15. Draw a rectangle with four rows of circles and two columns of circles. How many circles are there in your rectangle?

SHOW YOUR WORK

1.4 Chapter Test

1. There are **37** oranges and **23** apples in the fruit basket. How many pieces of fruit are in the basket?

SHOW YOUR WORK

2. Johnny adds **55** chocolate chips to his cookie dough. He adds **15** more after mixing it together. How many chocolate chips did Johnny use in his cookie dough?

SHOW YOUR WORK

3. It snows **12** inches. **5** inches of the snow melts. Then it snows **8** more inches. How much snow is on the ground now?

SHOW YOUR WORK

1.4 | Chapter Test

4. Sarah swims **25** laps of freestyle and **35** laps of backstroke at swim practice. How many laps did she swim all together?

SHOW YOUR WORK

5. Frank uses **65** pages in his notebook before winter break. He uses more pages after winter break. He used a total of **85** pages of his notebook all together. How many pages did he use after winter break?

SHOW YOUR WORK

6. 17 - 9 = ___ Explain your mental strategy.

SHOW YOUR WORK

1.4 Chapter Test

7. 11 - 6 = ___ Explain your mental strategy.

SHOW YOUR WORK

8. 18 - 9 = ___ Explain your mental strategy.

SHOW YOUR WORK

9. 14 + 3 = ___ Explain your mental strategy.

SHOW YOUR WORK

10. 12 + 7 = ___ Explain your mental strategy.

SHOW YOUR WORK

1.4 Chapter Test

11. 13 + 8 = ___ Explain your mental strategy.

SHOW YOUR WORK

12. Is 17 an even number? Justify your thinking.

SHOW YOUR WORK

13. Is 14 an even number? Justify your thinking.

SHOW YOUR WORK

1.4 Chapter Test

14. Is there an even number of strawberries below? Justify your thinking.

SHOW YOUR WORK

15. Is there an even number of hot dogs below? Justify your thinking.

SHOW YOUR WORK

16. Write an equation to represent the total number of hearts below.

SHOW YOUR WORK

17. Write an equation to represent the total number of stars below.

SHOW YOUR WORK

18. Write an equation to represent the total number of diamonds below.

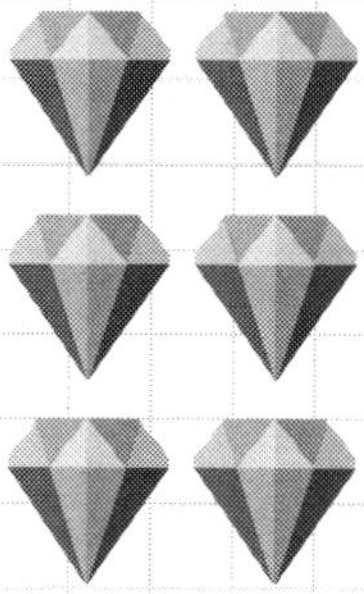

SHOW YOUR WORK

19. Draw a rectangle with five rows of circles and two columns of circles. How many circles are there in your rectangle?

SHOW YOUR WORK

20. Draw a rectangle with two rows of circles and three columns of circles. How many circles are there in your rectangle

SHOW YOUR WORK

Chapter 2:

Numbers & Operation in Base Ten

2.1. Understanding Three Digit Numbers page 58

2.2. Adding and Subtracting page 81

2.3. Chapter Test page 111

ARGOPREP

2.1.A | Understanding Three Digit Numbers

We already know that a group of 10 ones is a unit called a ten. In second grade, we also use a unit called a hundred. A hundred is a group of 10 tens. We can use groups of tens to help us count a large number of objects quickly. Let's look at an example.

Represent the number 312 using tens and ones.

We know that the number is read **three hundred** and **twelve**.

We need 10 tens for each one hundred, and there are 3 hundreds.

10 tens + 10 tens + 10 tens = 30 tens

We know that twelve is 1 ten and 2 ones.

1 Ten + 2 Ones

31 tens and 2 ones

NOTES

Practice Questions

1. Represent the number **107** using tens and ones.

_____ tens _____ ones

SHOW YOUR WORK

2. Represent the number **216** using tens and ones.

_____ tens _____ ones

SHOW YOUR WORK

3. Represent the number **314** using tens and ones.

_____ tens _____ ones

SHOW YOUR WORK

4. Represent the number 145 using tens and ones.

_____ tens _____ ones

SHOW YOUR WORK

5. Represent the number 324 using tens and ones.

_____ tens _____ ones

SHOW YOUR WORK

6. Represent the number 123 using tens and ones.

_____ tens _____ ones

SHOW YOUR WORK

7. Represent the number 165 using tens and ones.

_____ tens _____ ones

SHOW YOUR WORK

8. Represent the number 189 using tens and ones.

_____ tens _____ ones

SHOW YOUR WORK

9. Represent the number 235 using tens and ones.

_____ tens _____ ones

SHOW YOUR WORK

10. Represent the number **374** using tens and ones.

_____ tens _____ ones

SHOW YOUR WORK

11. How many tens are in the number **106**?

SHOW YOUR WORK

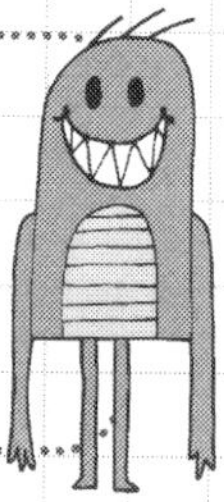

12. How many tens are in the number **326**?

SHOW YOUR WORK

13. How many tens are in the number 301?

SHOW YOUR WORK

14. What number represents the same amount as 2 hundreds + 12 tens + 3 ones?

SHOW YOUR WORK

15. What number represents the same amount as 34 hundreds + 16 tens + 5 ones?

SHOW YOUR WORK

Skip Counting

We can use what we know about grouping to count by 5s, 10s, and 100s. When we count by 5s, 10s, and 100s, we are counting groups of items with that amount in each group. This is called skip counting.

Skip counting helps us count a large number of objects more quickly.

Counting by 5s	Counting 10s	Counting 100s
The ones digit alternates between 5 and 0 when we skip count by 5.	The tens digit is the only digit that changes, increasing by one number.	The hundreds digit is the only digit that changes, increasing by one number when we skip count by one hundred.
125 130 135 140 145	125 135 145 155 165	125 225 325 425 525

2.1.B | Understanding Three Digit Numbers

Let's look at an example.

Luna is counting the strawberries she picked at the farm. She is skip counting by **5**s. If she continues to skip count by **5**s, what three numbers will she count next?

5, 10, ____, ____, ____

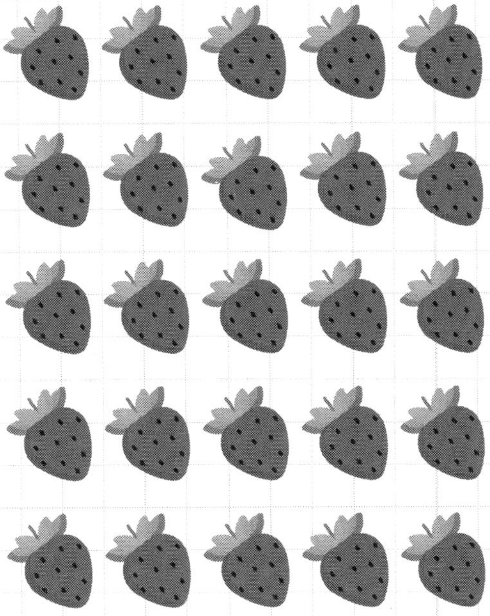

5

10

15

20

25

5, 10, 15, 20, 25

We can see that the ones digit alternates between **5** and **0** when we skip count by **5**.

Practice Questions

1. Lula is skip-counting counters by 5s. She's already counted 190 counters. If she continues to skip-count by 5s, what are the next 5 numbers she will count?

190, ____, ____, ____, ____, ____

SHOW YOUR WORK

2. Carla is skip-counting counters by 10s. She's already counted 360 counters. If she continues to skip-count by 10s, what are the next 5 numbers she will count?

360, ____, ____, ____, ____, ____

SHOW YOUR WORK

3. Hannah is skip-counting counters by 100s. She's already counted 275 counters. If she continues to skip-count by 100s, what are the next 5 numbers she will count?

275, ____, ____, ____, ____, ____

SHOW YOUR WORK

4. Count by 5s starting at 185. Fill in the blanks

185, ____, ____, ____, ____

SHOW YOUR WORK

5. Count by 10s starting at 185. Fill in the blanks

185, ____, ____, ____, ____

SHOW YOUR WORK

6. Count by 100s starting at 185. Fill in the blanks

185, ____, ____, ____, ____

SHOW YOUR WORK

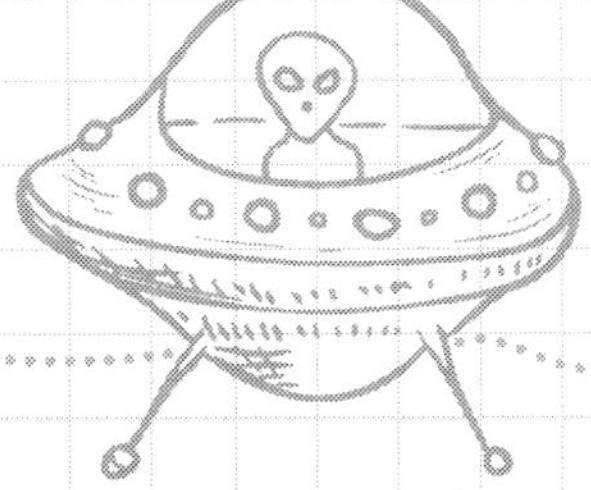

7. When counting by 5s from 285 to 385, which number would you not say?

A. 290

B. 300

C. 307

SHOW YOUR WORK

8. When counting by 10s from 285 to 385, which number would you not say?

A. 295

B. 300

C. 305

SHOW YOUR WORK

9. When counting by 100s from 285 to 585, which number would you not say?

A. 385

B. 485

C. 555

SHOW YOUR WORK

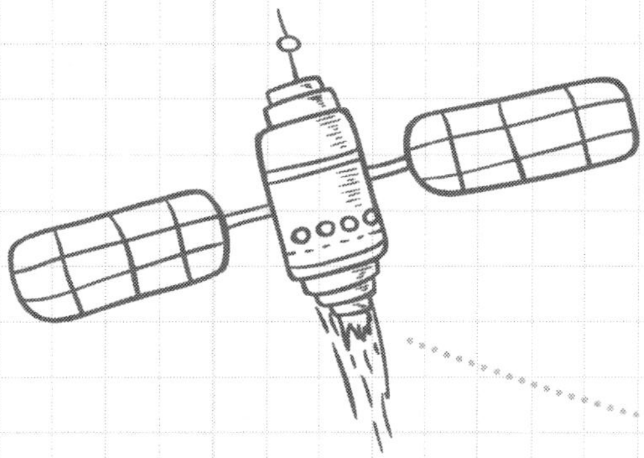

10. Fill in the blanks by counting backwards by 100s.

490, ____, ____, 190

SHOW YOUR WORK

11. Fill in the blanks by counting backwards by 10s.

555, ____, 535, ____, ____

SHOW YOUR WORK

12. Fill in the blanks by counting backwards by 5s.

375, ____, ____, 360, ____

SHOW YOUR WORK

13. Fill in the blanks by counting backwards by 100s.

660, ____, ____, 360

SHOW YOUR WORK

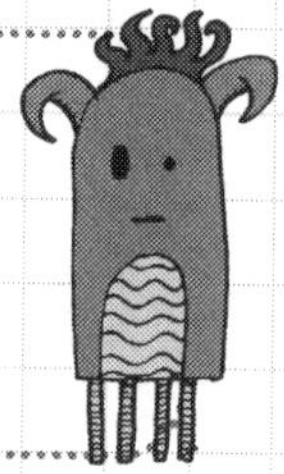

14. Fill in the blanks by counting backwards by 10s.

680, ____, 660, ____, ____

SHOW YOUR WORK

15. Fill in the blanks by counting backwards by 5s.

860, ____, ____, ____, ____

SHOW YOUR WORK

Creating Three-Digit Numbers

You can express three-digit numbers in different ways. Let's look at the number **456**. The number is expressed using base ten numerals, but we can rewrite it using expanded form or number names.

Expanded Form

To write a number in expanded form, we show each digit with its place value. It can be helpful to use the place value chart as a reference.

456

Place Value Chart		
hundreds	tens	ones

→

Place Value Chart		
hundreds	tens	ones
4	5	6

400 + 50 + 6

456 is expressed in expanded form as **400 + 50 + 6**

Number Names

When we write a number in word form, we use words instead of numbers. Let's look at **456** again.

456

Place Value Chart		
hundreds	tens	ones
4	5	6

↓ Four hundred ↓ fifty ↓ six

456 is expressed using number names as four hundred fifty-six.

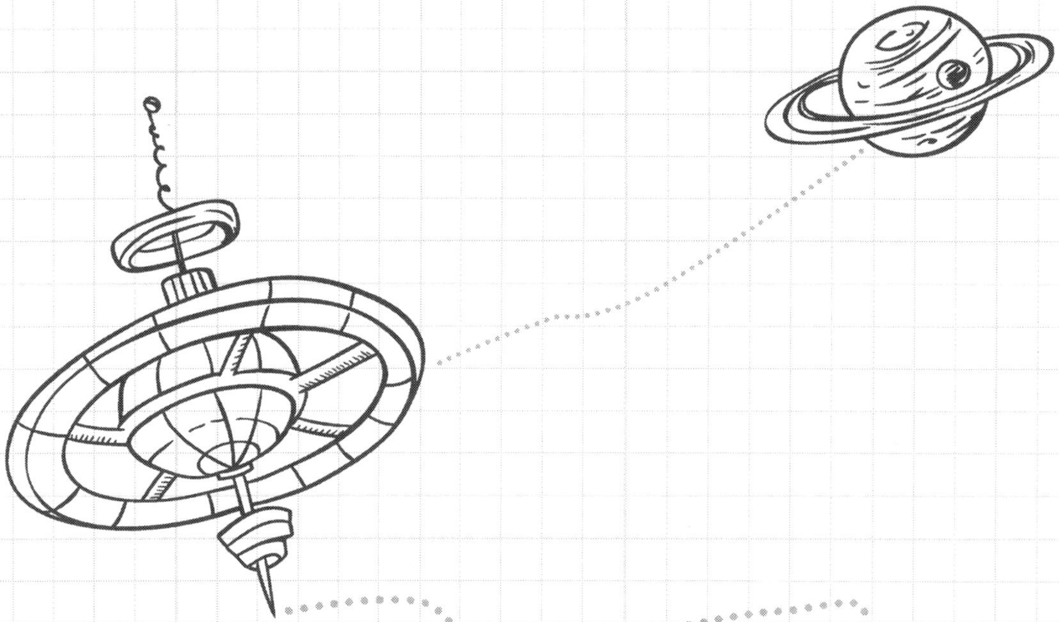

Practice Questions

1. Which expression represents the same amount as 515?

A. 500 + 10 + 5

B. 500 + 15 + 5

C. 51 + 5

SHOW YOUR WORK

2. Which expression represents the same amount as 888?

A. Eight Hundred Eight

B. Eighty-Eight Hundred

C. Eight Hundred Eighty-Eight

SHOW YOUR WORK

3. Which expression represents the same amount as 236?

A. Two Hundred Thirty-Six

B. Twenty-Three Hundred Six

C. Twenty Thirty-Six

SHOW YOUR WORK

4. Which expression represents the same amount as 455?

A. Four Hundred Five

B. Four Hundred Fifty-Five

C. Forty-Five Hundred Five

SHOW YOUR WORK

5. Which expression represents the same amount as 126?

A. 100 + 20 + 6

B. 10 + 2 + 6

C. 1 + 2 + 6

SHOW YOUR WORK

6. Fill in the blanks to make the equation true.

127 = ____ hundreds + ____ tens + ____ ones

SHOW YOUR WORK

7. Fill in the blanks to make the equation true.

989 = ____ hundreds + ____ tens + ____ ones

SHOW YOUR WORK

8. Fill in the blanks to make the equation true.

117 = ____ hundreds + ____ tens + ____ ones

SHOW YOUR WORK

9. Fill in the blanks to make the equation true.

611 = ____ hundreds + ____ tens + ____ ones

SHOW YOUR WORK

10. Fill in the blanks to make the equation true.

647 = ____ hundreds + ____ tens + ____ ones

SHOW YOUR WORK

11. Fill in the blanks to make the equation true.

____ = 2 hundreds + 3 tens + 5 ones

SHOW YOUR WORK

12. Fill in the blanks to make the equation true.

____ = 6 hundreds + 1 tens + 8 ones

SHOW YOUR WORK

13. Fill in the blanks to make the equation true.

____ = 5 hundreds + 4 tens + 15 ones

SHOW YOUR WORK

14. Fill in the blanks to make the equation true.

____ = 400 + 10 + 5

SHOW YOUR WORK

15. Fill in the blanks to make the equation true.

____ = 800 + 2

SHOW YOUR WORK

Comparing Three Digit Numbers

1. 304 ____ 340

A. >

B. <

C. =

SHOW YOUR WORK

2. 200 ____ 20 tens

A. >

B. <

C. =

SHOW YOUR WORK

3. 614 ____ 641

A. >

B. <

C. =

SHOW YOUR WORK

4. 400 + 10 + 2 ____ 400 + 9

A. >

B. <

C. =

SHOW YOUR WORK

5. 285 ____ 200 + 80 + 5

A. >

B. <

C. =

SHOW YOUR WORK

6. 919 ____ 991

A. >

B. <

C. =

SHOW YOUR WORK

7. 100 + 20 + 1 ____ 12 tens

A. >

B. <

C. =

SHOW YOUR WORK

8. 10 tens ____ 100 ones

A. >

B. <

C. =

SHOW YOUR WORK

9. 483 - 100 ____ 283 ones

A. >

B. <

C. =

SHOW YOUR WORK

10. Order the numbers from least to greatest: **266, 206, 244, 26**

_____ , _____ , _____ , _____

SHOW YOUR WORK

11. Order the numbers from least to greatest: **62, 116, 611, 66**

_____ , _____ , _____ , _____

SHOW YOUR WORK

12. Order the numbers from least to greatest: **25, 205, 485, 66**

_____ , _____ , _____ , _____

SHOW YOUR WORK

13. Order the numbers from least to greatest: **52, 520, 502, 25**

_____ , _____ , _____ , _____

SHOW YOUR WORK

14. Order the numbers from least to greatest: **642, 42, 24, 406**

_____ , _____ , _____ , _____

SHOW YOUR WORK

15. Order the numbers from least to greatest: **732, 32, 23, 723**

_____ , _____ , _____ , _____

SHOW YOUR WORK

2.2.A | Adding and Subtracting

We can use a variety of strategies to add and subtract large numbers. Let's look at an example

$$35 + 42 = \_\_\_$$

We can add these numbers more easily by using what we know about place value to break them into tens and ones.

Step 1: Break the numbers into tens and ones

$$35 + 42 = \_\_\_\_$$

$$30 + 5 + 40 + 2 = \_\_\_\_$$

Step 2: Add the tens

$$30 + 40 = 70$$

Step 3: Add the ones

$$5 + 2 = 7$$

Step 4: Combine the sums

$$70 + 7 = 77$$

ARGOPREP

2.2.A | Adding and Subtracting

Practice Questions

1. 56 + 35 = ____ Show your work.

SHOW YOUR WORK

2. 49 + 12 = ____ Show your work.

SHOW YOUR WORK

3. 62 + 26 = ____ Show your work.

SHOW YOUR WORK

4. 23 + 45 = ____ Show your work.

SHOW YOUR WORK

5. 33 + 63 = ____ Show your work.

SHOW YOUR WORK

6. 54 - 12 = ____ Show your work.

SHOW YOUR WORK

7. 62 - 12 = ____ Show your work.

SHOW YOUR WORK

8. 45 - 13 = ____ Show your work.

SHOW YOUR WORK

9. 50 - 12 = ____ Show your work.

SHOW YOUR WORK

10. 88 - 54 = ____ Show your work.

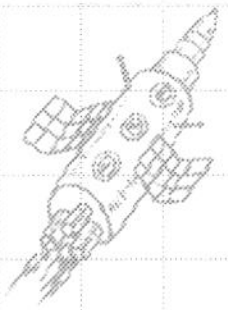

SHOW YOUR WORK

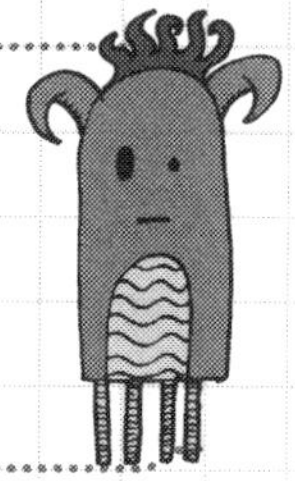

11. There are 46 kids at the birthday party. 25 more kids arrive. How many kids are at the party? Show your work.

SHOW YOUR WORK

12. Joe brings 52 cupcakes to the party. Sarah brings 45 more cupcakes to the party. How cupcakes are at the party? Show your work.

SHOW YOUR WORK

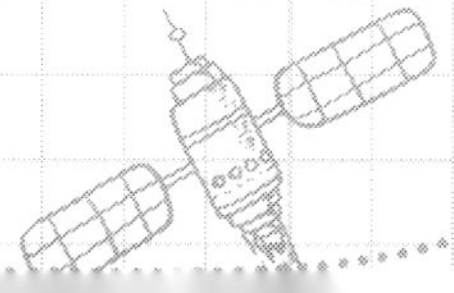

13. Sam bakes 78 cookies. His brother eats 35 of the cookies. How many cookies are left? Show your work.

SHOW YOUR WORK

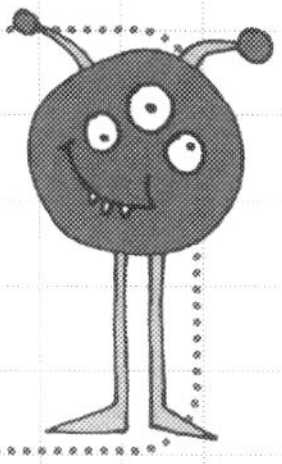

14. Linus collects 36 apples. He gives away 24 apples. How many apples does he have left? Show your work.

SHOW YOUR WORK

15. Nolan brings 90 pencils to school. He gives 45 of the pencils away. How many pencils does he have left? Show your work.

SHOW YOUR WORK

ARGOPREP

2.2.B | Adding Strings of Numbers

Adding Strings of Numbers

Adding strings of numbers can seem tricky, but we can reorder and combine the numbers in ways that make adding easier.

For example:

$$3\underline{2} + 15 + 2\underline{8} = \_\_\_\_$$

We know that 8 + 2 = 10. So, we can add 32 and 28 first. According to the associative property, the order we add numbers does not matter.

$$32 + 28 = 60$$

Now we can split 15 into tens and ones to add it to 60.

$$10 + 5 + 60 = 75$$

$$32 + 15 + 28 = 75 \checkmark$$

Practice Questions

1. 43 + 21 + 62 + 32 = ____ Show your work

SHOW YOUR WORK

2. 12 + 56 + 23 = ____ Show your work

SHOW YOUR WORK

3. 72 + 32 + 12 + 19 = ____ Show your work

SHOW YOUR WORK

4. 43 + 47 + 24 = ____ Show your work

SHOW YOUR WORK

ARGOPREP

2.2.B Adding Strings of Numbers

5. 39 + 64 + 32 + 15 = ____ Show your work

SHOW YOUR WORK

6. 35 + 23 + 76 = ____ Show your work

SHOW YOUR WORK

7. 24 + 38 + 54 = ____ Show your work

SHOW YOUR WORK

8. 25 + 37 + 32 + 19 = ____ Show your work

SHOW YOUR WORK

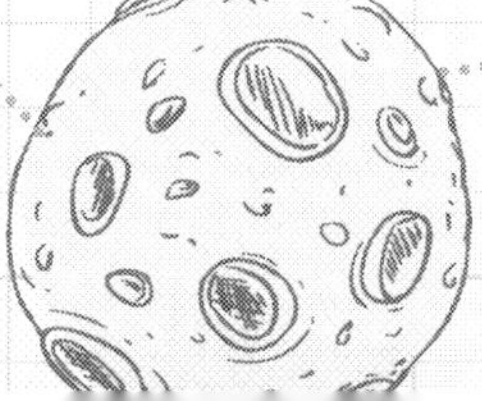

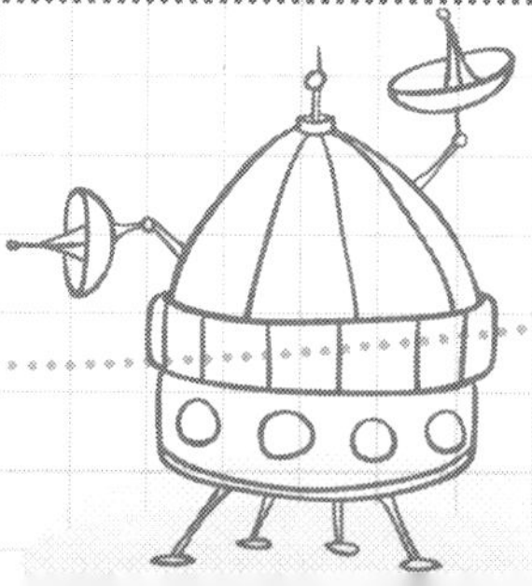

2.2.B | Adding Strings of Numbers

9. 67 + 26 + 39 + 15 = ____ Show your work

SHOW YOUR WORK

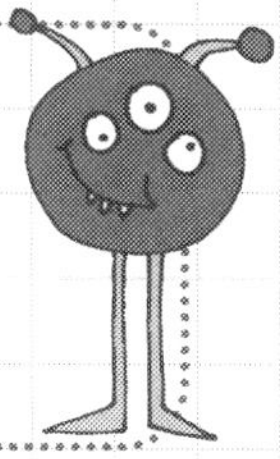

10. 42 + 27 + 32 = ____ Show your work

SHOW YOUR WORK

11. 45 + 28 + 13 + 87 = ____ Show your work

SHOW YOUR WORK

12. 47 + 29 + 14 = ____ Show your work

SHOW YOUR WORK

2.2B | Adding Strings of Numbers

13. John is taking a road trip. He drove **56** miles the first day, **35** miles the second day and **78** miles the third day. How many miles did he drive? Show your work.

SHOW YOUR WORK

14. Sarah is buying cupcakes for a party. She buys **35** vanilla cupcakes, **23** chocolate cupcakes, **47** carrot cake cupcakes and **26** spice cupcakes. How many cupcakes did she buy?

SHOW YOUR WORK

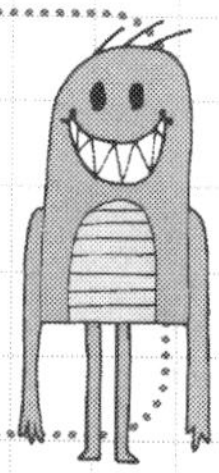

15. Joe bought **42** notebooks, **74** pencils and **46** erasers for his students. How many school supplies did he buy?

SHOW YOUR WORK

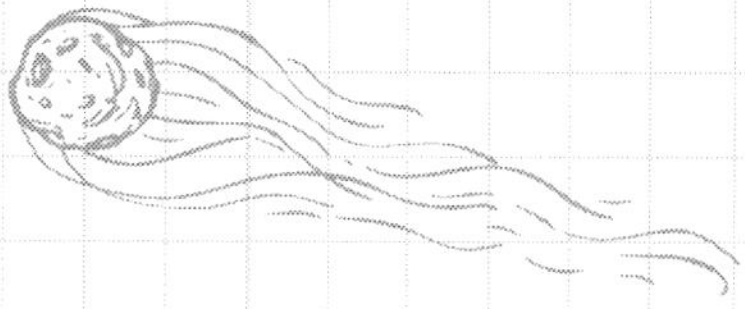

Add and Subtract within 1,000

We can use what we know about place value to add and subtract large numbers. For example:

$$387 - 204 = \_\_\_\_$$

Step One: Look at the value of each digit. You can use a place value chart to help you see the value of each digit

Place Value Chart		
hundreds	tens	ones
3	8	7

Place Value Chart		
hundreds	tens	ones
2	0	4

Step Two: Subtract the 100s, 10s and 1s.

Place Value Chart		
hundreds	tens	ones
1	8	3

387 - 204 = 183

We can use models to check our work. Let's use place value blocks.

387 - 204 = 183

Step One: Represent the first number using the place value blocks

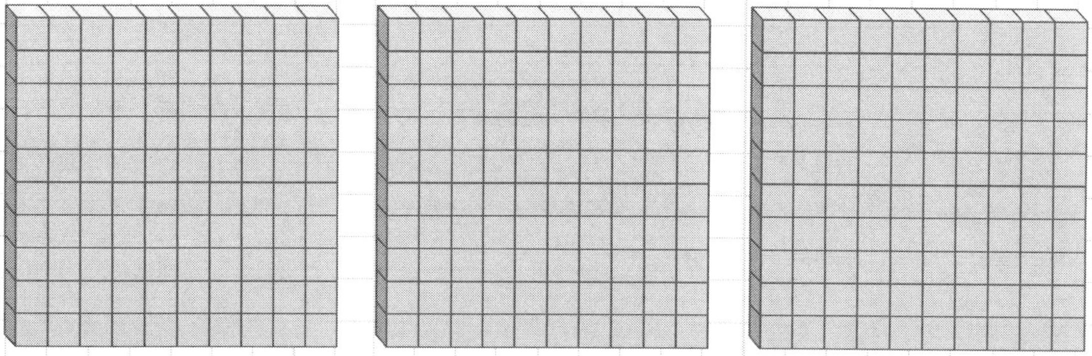

3 hundreds

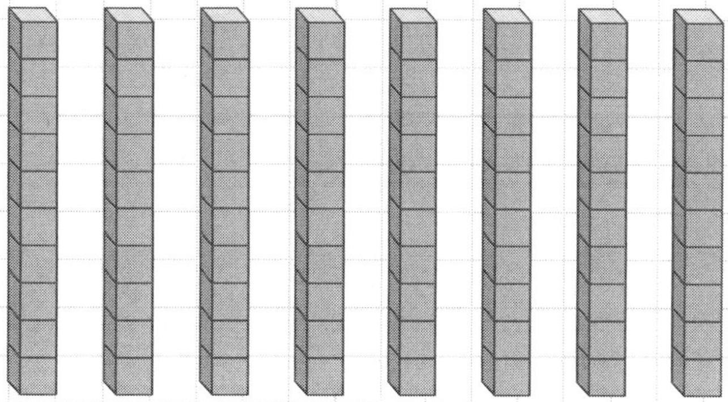

8 tens

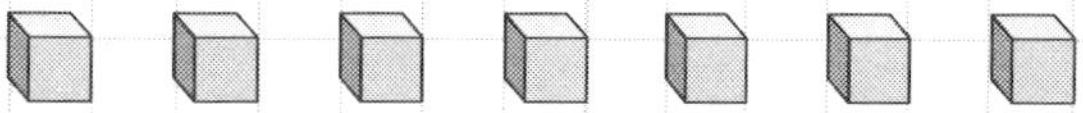

7 ones

Step Two: Subtract by crossing

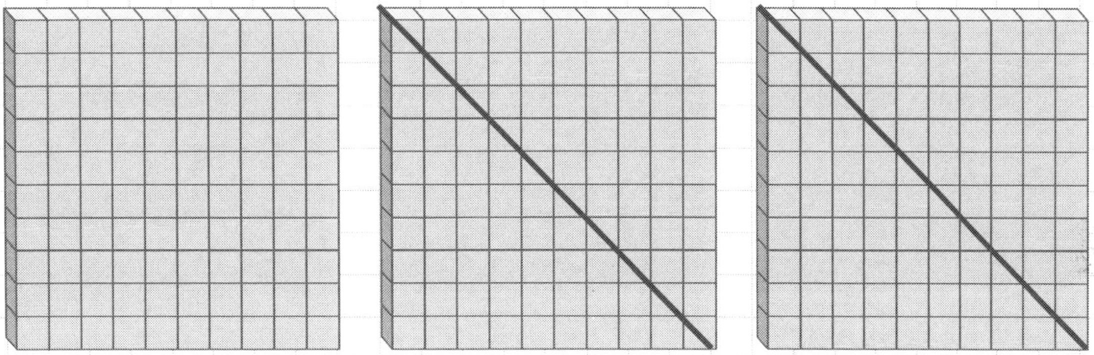

minus 2 hundreds

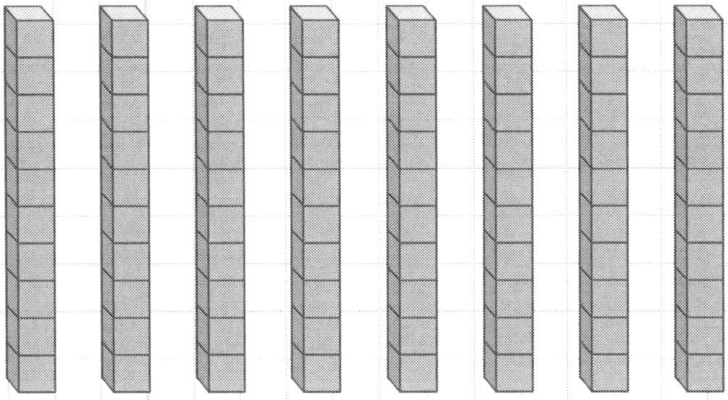

minus 0 tens

minus 4 ones

Step Three: Count the remaining blocks

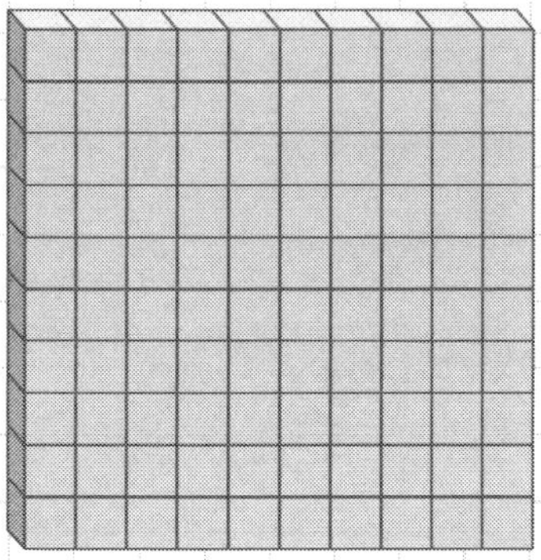

1 hundred

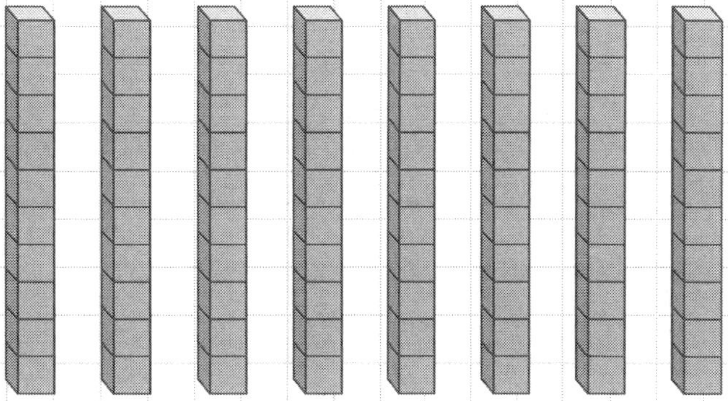

8 tens

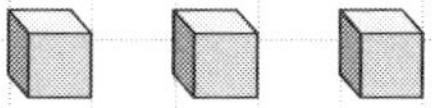

3 ones

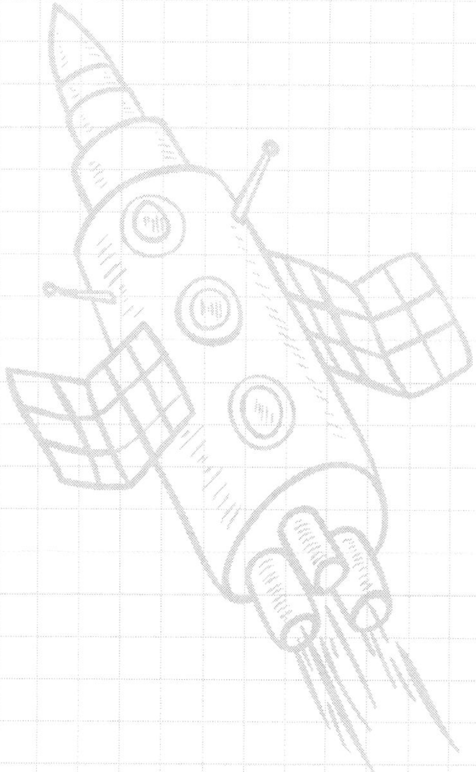

387 - 204 = 183 ✓

Practice Questions

1. Which of the following represents 314 + 416

A. 7 hundreds + 3 tens

B. 7 hundreds + 2 tens + 9 ones

C. 4 hundreds + 3 tens + 10 ones

SHOW YOUR WORK

2. Which of the following represents 504 + 214

A. 500 + 20 + 10 + 4 + 4

B. 500 + 200 + 10 + 4 + 4

C. 500 + 200 + 40 + 10 + 4

SHOW YOUR WORK

3. Which problem is the same as 234 + 543

A. 2 + 3 + 4 + 5 + 4 + 3

B. 200 + 300 + 30 + 30 + 4 + 4

C. 500 + 200 + 30 + 40 + 4 + 3

SHOW YOUR WORK

4. 543 - 234 = ____ Use a model to show your thinking.

SHOW YOUR WORK

5. 194 - 123 = ____ Use a model to show your thinking.

SHOW YOUR WORK

6. 274 - 112 - ____ Use a model to show your thinking.

SHOW YOUR WORK

7. 976 - 234 = ____ Use a model to show your thinking.

SHOW YOUR WORK

8. 786 - 346 = ____ Use a model to show your thinking.

SHOW YOUR WORK

9. 123 + 321 = ____ Use a model to show your thinking.

SHOW YOUR WORK

10. 334 + 623 = ____ Use a model to show your thinking.

SHOW YOUR WORK

11. 294 + 234 = ____ Use a model to show your thinking.

SHOW YOUR WORK

12. 157 + 643 = ____ Use a model to show your thinking.

SHOW YOUR WORK

13. Hattie is stacking blocks. She stacks 587 blocks. Her brother knocks down 123 blocks. How many blocks are left in the stack?

SHOW YOUR WORK

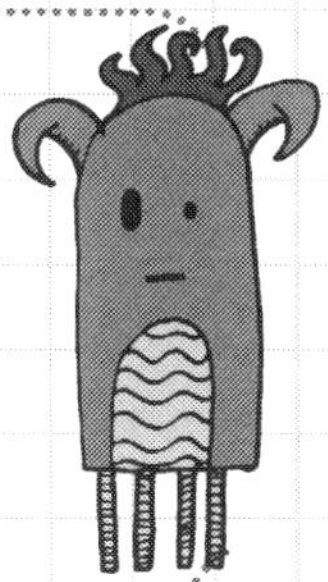

14. Aldous is collecting seashells. He gathers 327 shells during his first summer. He gathers 432 more shells the next summer. How many shells did Aldous gather for his collection?

SHOW YOUR WORK

15. Adele spills 837 specks of glitter on the floor. She picks up 234 specks of glitter. Her friend picks up another 432 specks of glitter. How many specks of glitter are still on the ground?

SHOW YOUR WORK

ARGOPREP

2.2.D | Adding and Subtracting

Mentally Adding and Subtracting 10s and 100s

We can use what we know about place value and skip counting to add and subtract by 10s and 100s. We can do this quickly without showing our work. Let's look at the number 425.

Adding and Subtracting by 10s	Adding and Subtracting by 100s
With addition, the tens digit increases.	With addition, the hundreds digit increases.
425	425
435	525
445	625
With subtraction, the tens digit decreases.	With subtraction, the hundreds digit decreases.
425	425
415	325
405	225

Practice Questions

1. 843 - 10 = ____

SHOW YOUR WORK

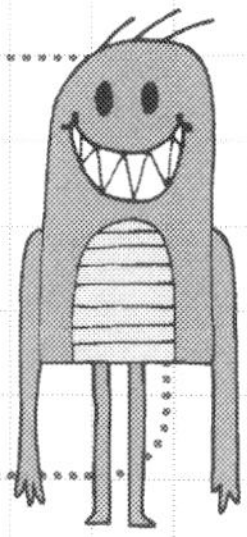

2. 672 + 30 = ____

SHOW YOUR WORK

3. 543 - 400 = ____

SHOW YOUR WORK

4. 713 + 100 = ____

SHOW YOUR WORK

5. 605 - 200 = ____

SHOW YOUR WORK

6. 810 + 100 = ____

SHOW YOUR WORK

7. 929 - 10 = ____

SHOW YOUR WORK

8. What is 30 more than 507?

SHOW YOUR WORK

9. What is 200 more than 260?

SHOW YOUR WORK

10. What is 10 less than 912?

SHOW YOUR WORK

11. What is 100 less than 912?

SHOW YOUR WORK

12. What is 50 more than 311?

SHOW YOUR WORK

13. What is 100 more than 243?

SHOW YOUR WORK

14. What is 20 less than 122?

SHOW YOUR WORK

15. What is 100 less than 422?

SHOW YOUR WORK

NOTES

Explaining Different Strategies

We've learned several strategies for adding and subtracting large numbers. It's important to understand why each strategy works. Let's look at an example.

There are 35 students at the pool. 22 more students arrive at the pool after snack time. Then, 15 more students arrive at the pool after lunch. How many students are at the pool now?

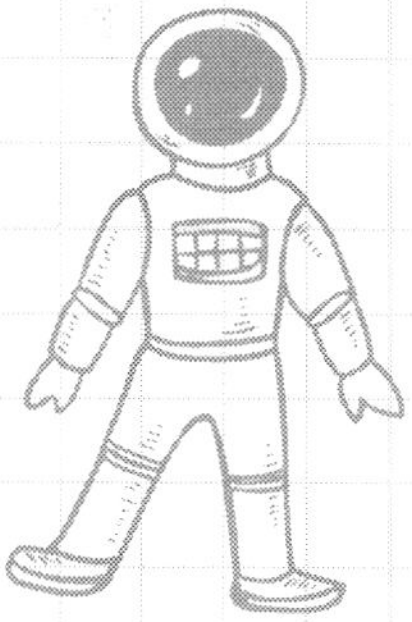

Step One: Determine what the problem is asking you to do
We can see that this is an addition problem.

$$35 + 22 + 15 = \_\_\_\_$$

Step Two: Choose a Strategy
There is more than one way to solve this problem.

Strategy One

We can use number relationships and reorder the numbers in the equation.

$$35 + 22 + 15 = \_\_\_\_$$

We know that 5 + 5 is 10.
So, we can add 35 and 15 first.

$$35 + 15 = 50$$

$$50 + 22 = 72$$

Strategy Two

We look at place value and break the numbers into tens and ones.

$$35 + 22 + 15 = \_\_\_\_$$

$$30 + 20 + 10 = 60$$

$$5 + 2 + 5 = 12$$

$$60 + 12 = 72$$

Step Three: Explain why the strategy works

Both strategies give us the same answer. Why does this work?

$$35 + 22 + 15 = 72$$

Strategy One

Rearranging the numbers works because this is an addition problem.

We know that changing the order of the numbers does not change the solution of an addition problem.

Strategy Two

Breaking the numbers up into tens and ones works because we added up all the tens and then added up the ones. We also combined the sums.

Since we didn't leave out any part of the problem, we arrived at the correct answer.

NOTES

Practice Questions

1. 54 - 25 = ____ Explain your strategy.

SHOW YOUR WORK

2. 62 - 17 = ____ Explain your strategy.

SHOW YOUR WORK

3. 82 - 41 = ____ Explain your strategy.

SHOW YOUR WORK

4. 44 - 22 - 13 = ____ Explain your strategy.

SHOW YOUR WORK

5. 94 - 62 - 10 = ____ Explain your strategy.

SHOW YOUR WORK

6. 63 + 45 = ____ Explain your strategy.

SHOW YOUR WORK

7. 75 + 23 = ____ Explain your strategy.

SHOW YOUR WORK

8. 32 + 45 = ____ Explain your strategy.

SHOW YOUR WORK

9. 44 + 75 + 10 = ____ Explain your strategy.

SHOW YOUR WORK

10. 23 + 42 + 15 = ____ Explain your strategy.

SHOW YOUR WORK

11. Sarah picks 24 apples. Her brother picks 54 apples. How many apples do they pick all together? Show two ways to solve the problem

SHOW YOUR WORK

12. Simon drives 36 miles on Monday and 45 miles on Tuesday. He drives another 27 miles on Thursday. How many miles did he drive all together? Show two ways to solve the problem

SHOW YOUR WORK

13. Lauren spends **$23** on a new shirt, **$45** dollars on new pants and **$59** on new shoes. How much money did she spend all together? Show two ways to solve the problem.

SHOW YOUR WORK

14. Maria makes **82** cupcakes for the party. Her friends eat **37** of the cupcakes before dinner. How many cupcakes does she have left? Show two ways to solve the problem.

SHOW YOUR WORK

15. Tim has **95** flowers. He gives away **54** of his flowers. How many flowers does he have left? Show two ways to solve the problem.

SHOW YOUR WORK

ARGOPREP

2.3 | Chapter Test

1. Represent the number **217** using tens and ones.

_____ tens _____ ones

SHOW YOUR WORK

2. What number represents the same amount as **3** hundreds + **11** tens + **2** ones?

SHOW YOUR WORK

3. Count by **100**s starting at **655**. Fill in the blanks

655, ____, ____, ____

SHOW YOUR WORK

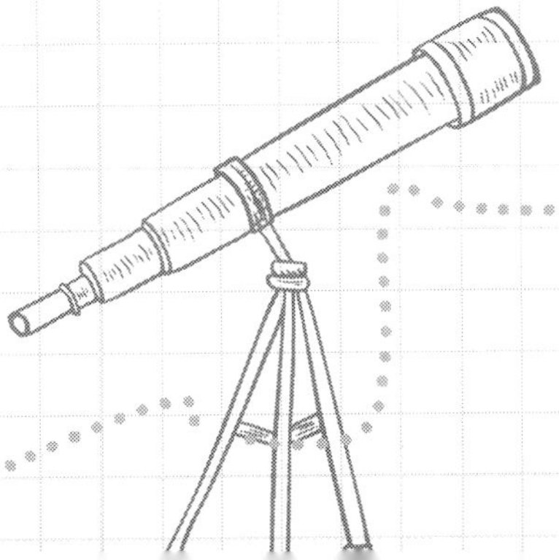

2.3 | Chapter Test

4. Count by 10s starting at **655**. Fill in the blanks

655, ____, ____, ____

SHOW YOUR WORK

5. Count by 5s starting at **655**. Fill in the blanks

655, ____, ____, ____

SHOW YOUR WORK

6. Fill in the blanks to make the equation true.

____ = **5** hundreds + **12** tens + **2** ones

SHOW YOUR WORK

2.3 Chapter Test

7. Which expressions represent the same amount as 276?

A. 2 + 7 + 6

B. 20 + 7 + 6

C. 200 + 70 + 6

SHOW YOUR WORK

8. 854 ____ 845

A. >

B. <

C. =

SHOW YOUR WORK

9. 100 + 5 ____ 10 tens + 5 ones

A. >

B. <

C. =

SHOW YOUR WORK

10. Order the numbers from least to greatest: 17, 702, 107, 71

____ , ____ , ____ , ____

SHOW YOUR WORK

11. What is 100 less than 312?

SHOW YOUR WORK

12. 63 + 47 = ____

SHOW YOUR WORK

2.3 | Chapter Test

13. There are 94 kids at the pool. 32 kids leave. How many kids remain at the pool?

SHOW YOUR WORK

14. What is 200 more than 212?

SHOW YOUR WORK

15. What is 30 less than 583?

SHOW YOUR WORK

16. 33 + 14 + 55 + 36 = ____

SHOW YOUR WORK

2.3 Chapter Test

17. 75 + 64 + 25 + 16 = ____

SHOW YOUR WORK

18. 553 - 131 = ____ Show your work.

SHOW YOUR WORK

19. 326 - 124 = ____ Show your work.

SHOW YOUR WORK

20. The chickens lay 23 eggs in the morning. They lay 47 more in the afternoon and 56 more before nightfall. How many eggs did the chickens lay in all? Explain your strategy for solving the problem.

SHOW YOUR WORK

NOTES

Chapter 3:
Measurement & Data

3.1. Using Tools to Measure page 120

3.2. Using Addition and Subtraction to Solve Word Problems page 147

3.3. Working with Time and Money page 162

3.4. Represent Data page 176

3.5. Chapter Test page 192

ARGOPREP

3.1.A | Using Tools to Measure

We can use a variety of tools to measure objects. Most of the time, we will use a ruler, yardstick, meter stick or measuring tape.

Using a Ruler

A ruler can be used to measure lengths in inches (in) or centimeters (cm). The centimeters are marked along the top of the ruler. The inches are marked along the bottom of the ruler.

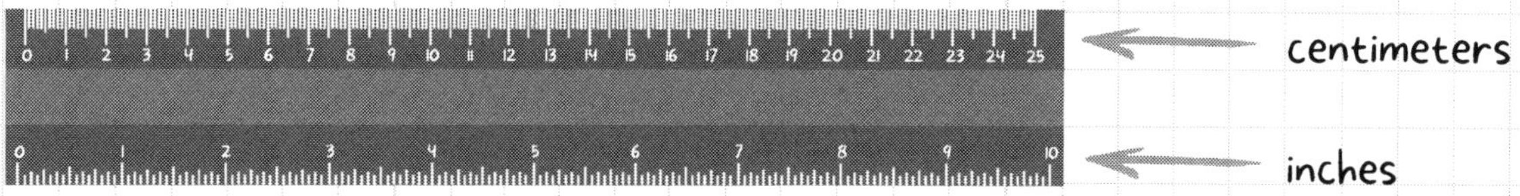

To measure objects with a ruler, place one end of the object at the zero hash mark of the ruler. Place the rest of the object along the edge of the ruler, without any gaps.

Let's use a pencil as an example. Notice that the tip of the pencil is placed just under the zero hash mark, and the rest of the pencil is lined up alongside the ruler.

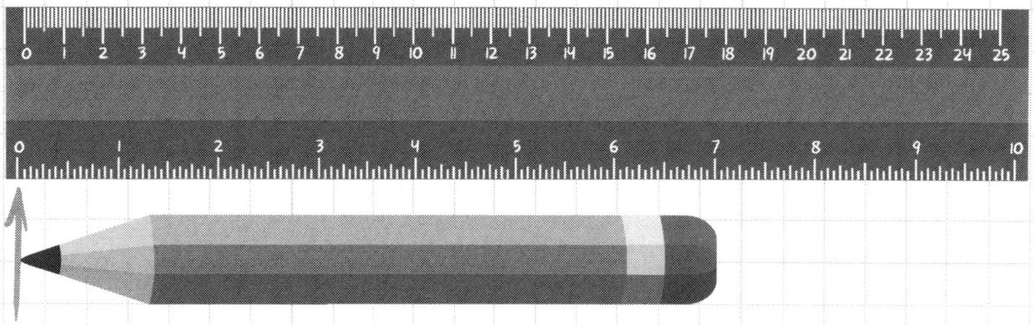

3.1.A | Using Tools to Measure

To determine the length, read the hashmark where the object ends. For example, the pencil is 7 inches long.

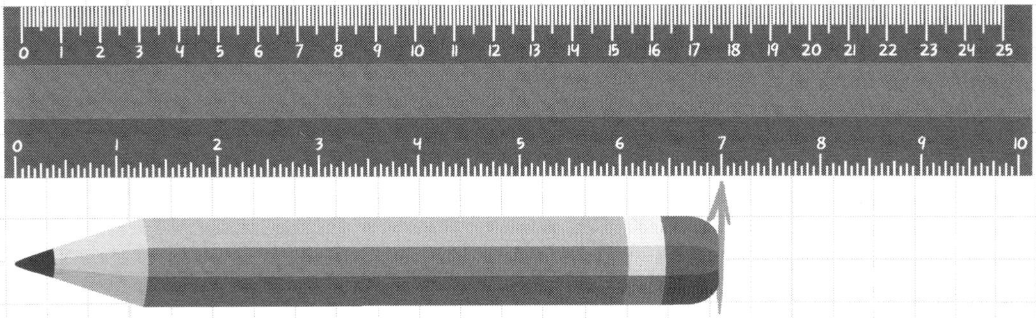

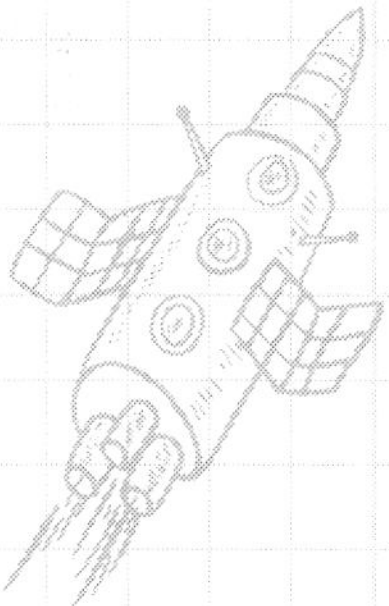

Other Tools for Measuring Length

Yardstick

A yardstick is 3 feet long. It can be used to measure lengths in inches or feet.

Meter Stick

The metric system uses a tool similar to a yardstick. It is called a meter stick. A meter stick is one meter long. It can be used to measure lengths in centimeters or millimeters.

Measuring Tape

Measuring tape is a flexible ruler. It can be used to measure lengths in centimeters, inches, and feet.

How do I know which tool to use?

The tool you use depends on the size of the object. For example, it would take a long time to measure the height of a door with a ruler. It is more efficient to use a longer tool, such as a yardstick or meter stick.

3.1.A | Using Tools to Measure

Practice Questions

1. Which tool would be most efficient when measuring the length of a school pencil?

A. ruler

B. yardstick

SHOW YOUR WORK

2. Which tool would be most efficient when measuring the length of a cafeteria table?

A. ruler

B. yardstick

SHOW YOUR WORK

3. Which tool would be most efficient when measuring the length of a sticky note?

A. ruler

B. yardstick

4. Which tool would be most efficient when measuring the length of a crayon?

A. ruler

B. yardstick

SHOW YOUR WORK

5. Which tool would be most efficient when measuring the length of a truck?

A. ruler

B. yardstick

SHOW YOUR WORK

6. Which image shows the correct way to measure the paper clip?

A.

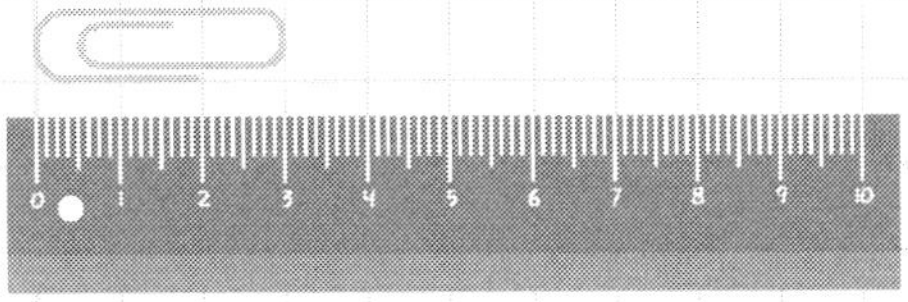

B.

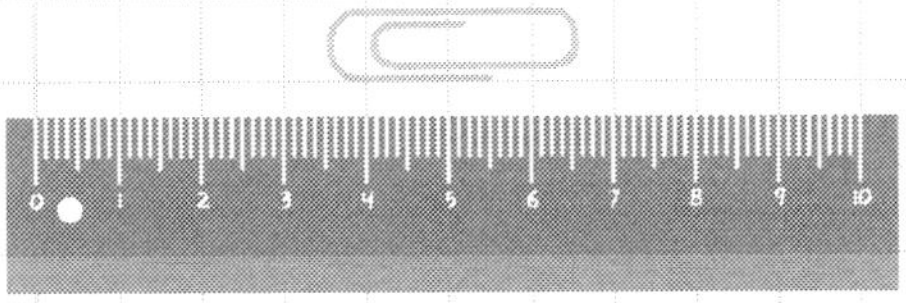

C.

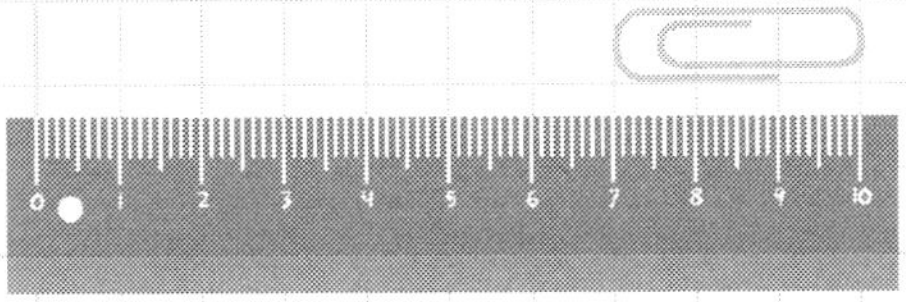

SHOW YOUR WORK

Use a ruler to complete questions 7 - 11

7. What is the height of the toy washing machine?

________ cm

SHOW YOUR WORK

8. What is the length of the tape dispenser?

________ cm

SHOW YOUR WORK

9. What is the length of the pencil?

________ cm

SHOW YOUR WORK

10. What is the height of the chair?

________ in

SHOW YOUR WORK

11. What is the height of the book?

SHOW YOUR WORK

________ in

Use your ruler and the rectangle below to answer questions 12 - 15

12. What is the length of Side A?

A. 2 cm

B. 4 cm

C. 2 in

D. 4 in

SHOW YOUR WORK

13. What is the length of Side B?

A. 9 cm

B. 12 cm

C. 9 in

D. 12 in

SHOW YOUR WORK

14. What is the length of Side C

A. 2 cm

B. 4 cm

C. 2 in

D. 4 in

SHOW YOUR WORK

15. What is the length of Side D

A. 9 cm

B. 12 cm

C. 9 in

D. 12 in

SHOW YOUR WORK

NOTES

Understanding Different Measurements

Objects can be measured using different units of length. For example, we could use a yardstick to measure the length of the fence in inches, feet or yards.

The fence is 3 yards long. How long is the fence in feet?

Conversion Chart
1 feet = 12 inches
1 yard = 3 feet
1 meter = 100 cm

We know the fence is 3 yards long ✓

We know that there are 3 feet in each yard ✓

3 feet + 3 feet + 3 feet = ____ feet

↑ ↑ ↑

1 yard 1 yard 1 yard = 3 feet

The fence is 9 feet long ✓

3.1.B | Using Tools to Measure

Practice Questions

Use a ruler and the image below to answer questions 1 - 3.

1. What is the height of the street lamp in inches?

A. 1 in

B. 1.5 in

C. 2 in

D. 2.5 in

SHOW YOUR WORK

2. What is the height of the street lamp in centimeters?

A. 1 cm

B. 1.5 cm

C. 2 cm

D. 2.5 cm

SHOW YOUR WORK

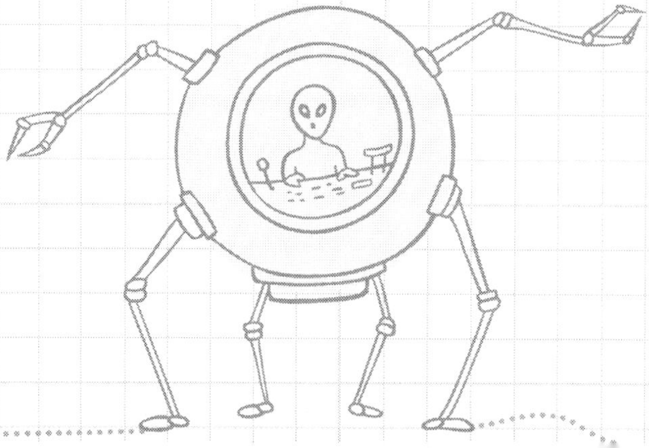

3. Why is the height bigger in centimeters than in inches?

SHOW YOUR WORK

Use a ruler and the image below to answer questions 4 - 6.

4. What is the height of the hydrant in inches?

A. 2 in

B. 3 in

C. 4 in

D. 5 in

SHOW YOUR WORK

5. What is the height of the hydrant in centimeters?

A. 2 cm

B. 3 cm

C. 4 cm

D. 5 cm

SHOW YOUR WORK

6. Why is the height bigger in centimeters than in inches?

SHOW YOUR WORK

7. The toy house is 2 feet long. How many inches long is the toy house?

A. 12 ft

B. 24 ft

C. 12 in

D. 24 in

SHOW YOUR WORK

8. The tower is 5 yards tall. How many feet is the tower?

A. 15 ft

B. 500 ft

C. 15 yards

D. 500 yards

SHOW YOUR WORK

9. The desk is 2 meters long. How many centimeters long is the desk?

A. 200 m

B. 20 m

C. 200 cm

D. 20 cm

SHOW YOUR WORK

10. The tree is 5 ft tall. How many inches tall is the tree?

A. 50 in

B. 60 in

C. 70 in

D. 80 in

SHOW YOUR WORK

11. John is 200 cm tall. How many meters tall is John?

A. 1 m

B. 2 m

C. 3 m

D. 4 m

SHOW YOUR WORK

12. The field is 7 yards. How many feet is the field?

_______ ft

SHOW YOUR WORK

13. The painting is 3 yards. How many feet is the painting?

_______ ft

SHOW YOUR WORK

14. Esther states that the height of the door is 3 yards. Jasmine states that the height of the door is 9 feet. Explain how the measurements can both be used to describe the height of the door.

SHOW YOUR WORK

15. The doctor tells Margie that she is 3 ft tall. The nurse tells Margie that she is **36** in tall. Explain how the measurements can both be used to describe Margie's height.

SHOW YOUR WORK

NOTES

Estimating Lengths

We can use what we know about length to estimate different measurements. Look at the example below.

About how long is the loaf of bread?

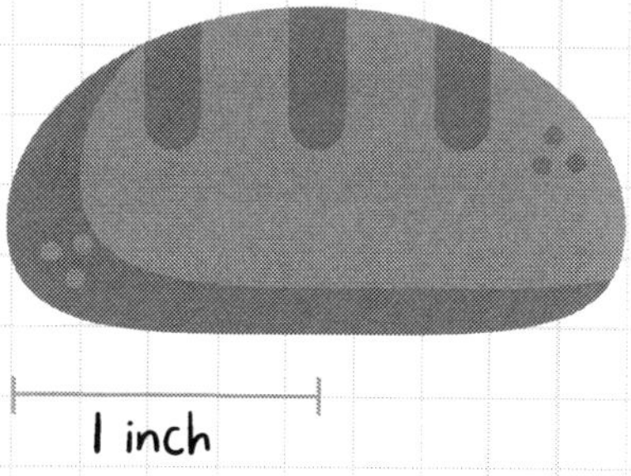

Let's look at the different parts of the problem.

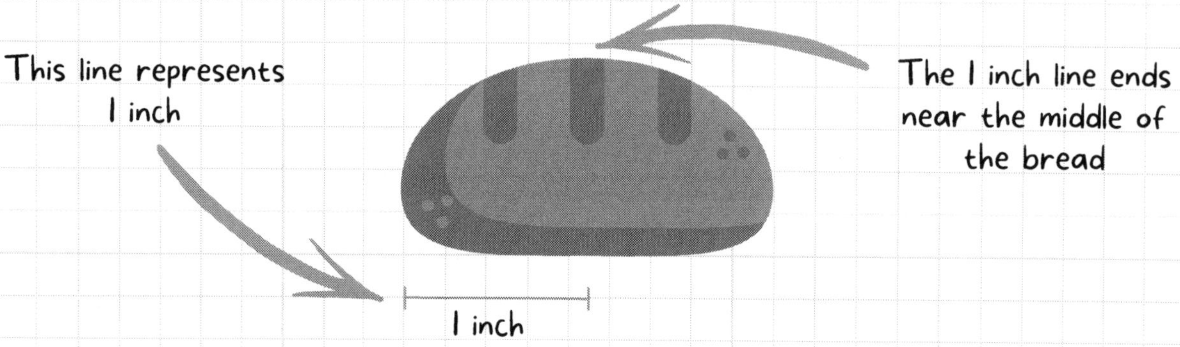

Since half of the bread is 1 inch, we know that the other half is also 1 inch because halves are always equal.
We can write the equation 1 + 1 = ____ inches

The loaf of bread is about 2 inches long ✓

Practice Questions

1. About how wide is the pumpkin?

A. 1 ft

B. 2 ft

C. 3 ft

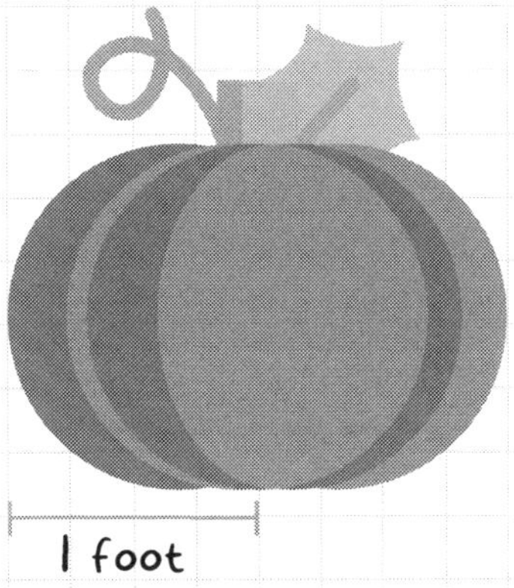

SHOW YOUR WORK

2. About how tall is the flower?

A. 2 in

B. 4 in

C. 6 in

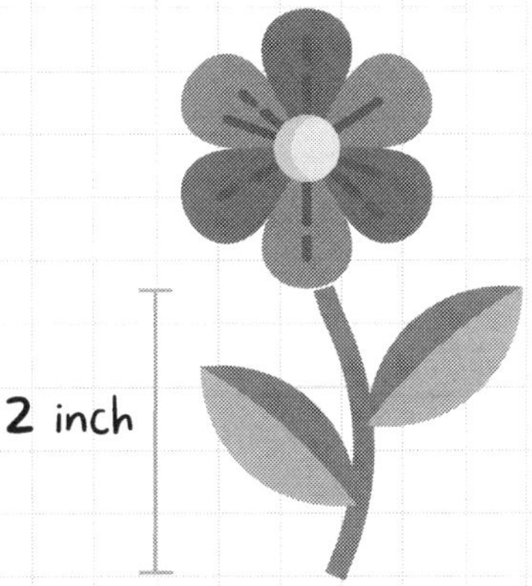

SHOW YOUR WORK

3. About how long is the bean?

A. 2 cm

B. 3 cm

C. 4 cm

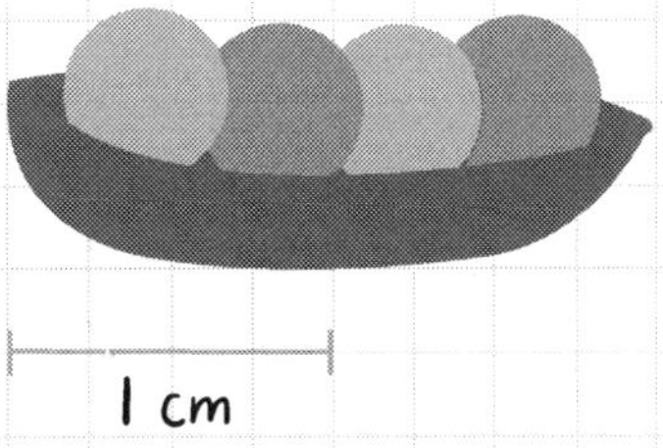

SHOW YOUR WORK

4. About how long is the caterpillar?

A. 2 cm

B. 4 cm

C. 6 cm

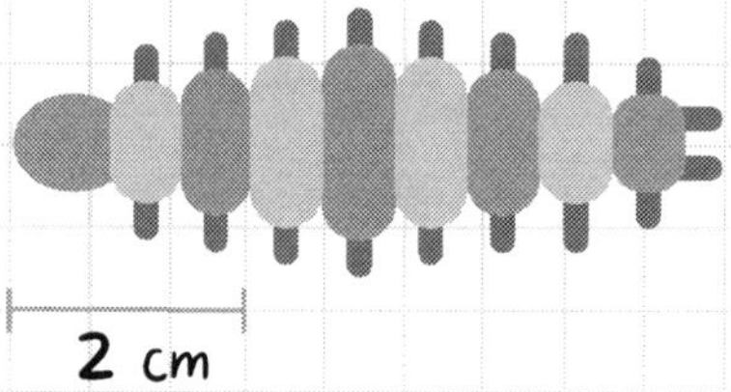

SHOW YOUR WORK

5. About how tall is the big water bottle?

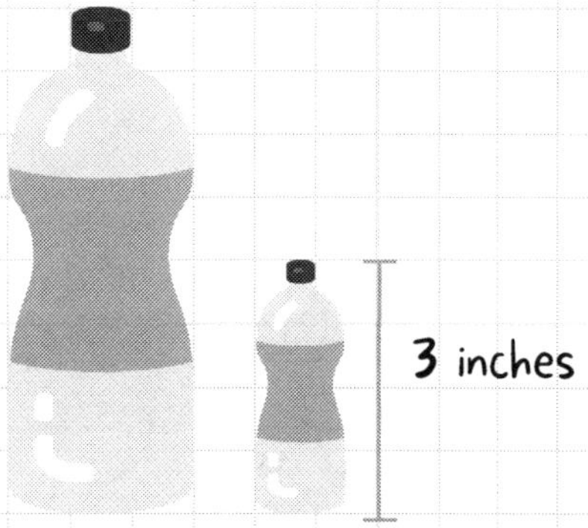

SHOW YOUR WORK

6. About how long is the small sandwich?

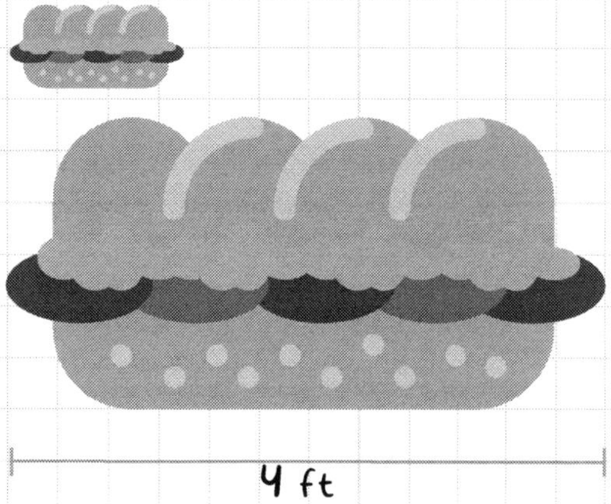

SHOW YOUR WORK

7. About how tall is the small stack of pancakes?

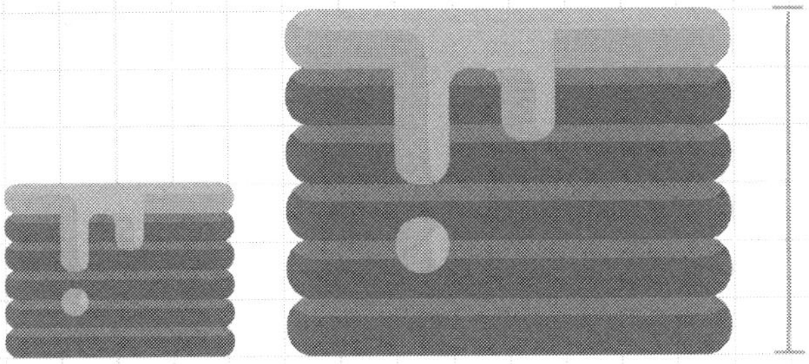

10 inches

SHOW YOUR WORK

8. About how tall is the big burger?

2 in

SHOW YOUR WORK

9. About how tall is the big flamingo?

1 ft

SHOW YOUR WORK

10. About how tall is the small stack of chips?

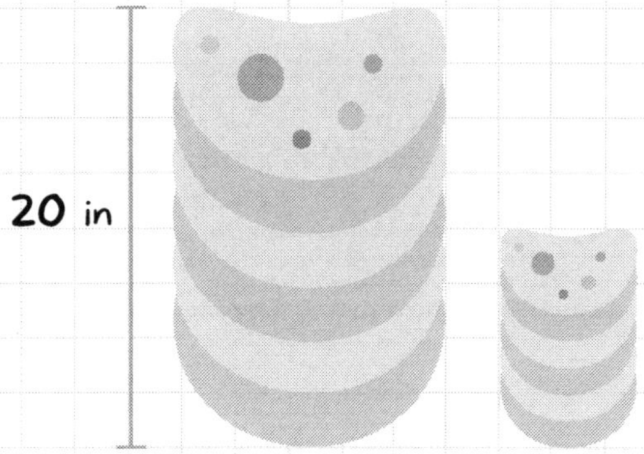

SHOW YOUR WORK

11. Which is the best length estimate for a swimming pool?

A. 25 centimeters

B. 25 inches

C. 25 meters

SHOW YOUR WORK

12. Which is the best length estimate for a building?

A. 50 centimeters

B. 50 inches

C. 50 feet

SHOW YOUR WORK

ARGOPREP

3.1.C Using Tools to Measure

13. Which is the best length estimate for a book?

A. 25 centimeters

B. 25 inches

C. 25 yards

SHOW YOUR WORK

14. Which is the best length estimate for a doorway?

A. 10 inches

B. 10 feet

C. 10 meters

SHOW YOUR WORK

15. Which is the best length estimate for a nail?

A. 10 centimeters

B. 10 inches

C. 10 meters

SHOW YOUR WORK

Comparing Measurements

There are times when we need to compare different lengths.

How much longer is Line B than Line A?

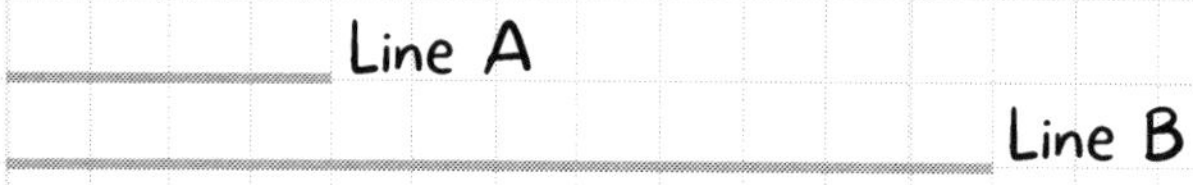

Step 1: Measure each line

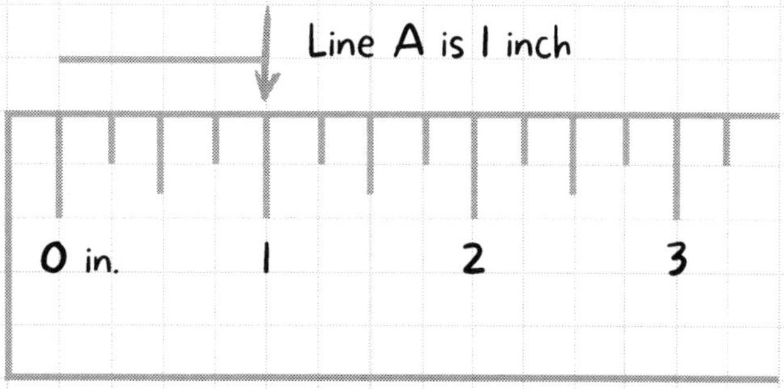

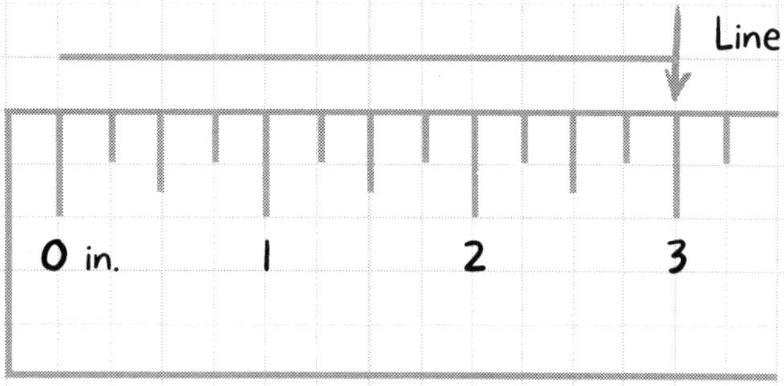

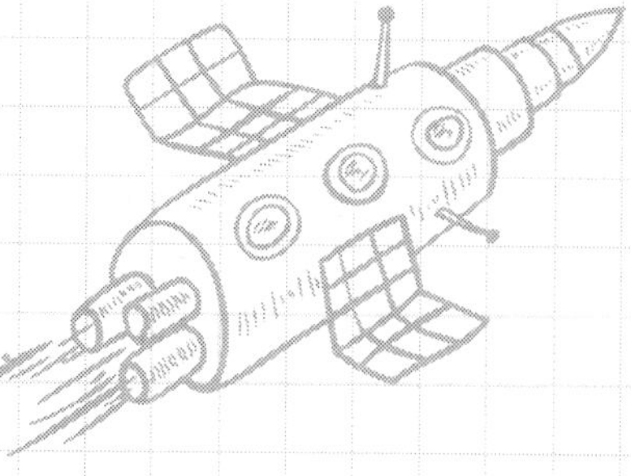

Step 2: Write an equation

We know that Line A is 1 inch. We also know that Line B is 3 inches. We need to find the **difference** between the two lines.

$$3 - 1 = \_\_\_\_$$

We could also look at the distance between the two hashmarks on the ruler.

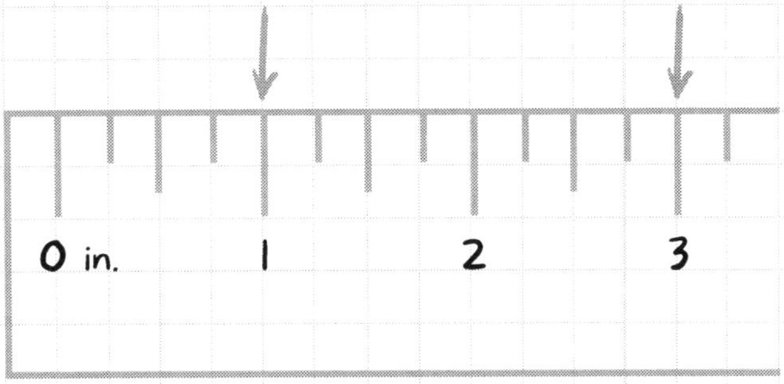

Step 3: Solve

$$3 - 1 = 2$$

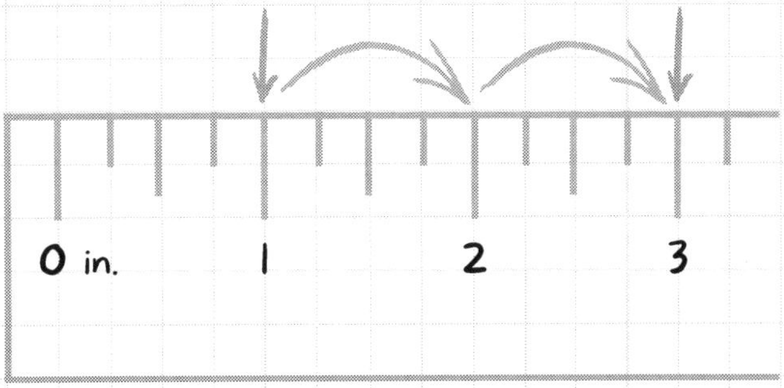

Line B is 2 inches longer than Line A ✓

3.1.D | Using Tools to Measure

Practice Questions

Use an inch ruler and the objects below to answer questions 1 - 3.

____________________________ Line A

____ Line B

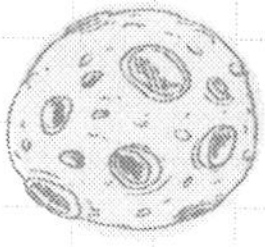

1. Line A is _____ inches long.

2. Line B is _____ inches long.

3. Line A is about _____ inches shorter than Line B

SHOW YOUR WORK

Use an inch ruler and the objects below to answer questions 4 - 8.

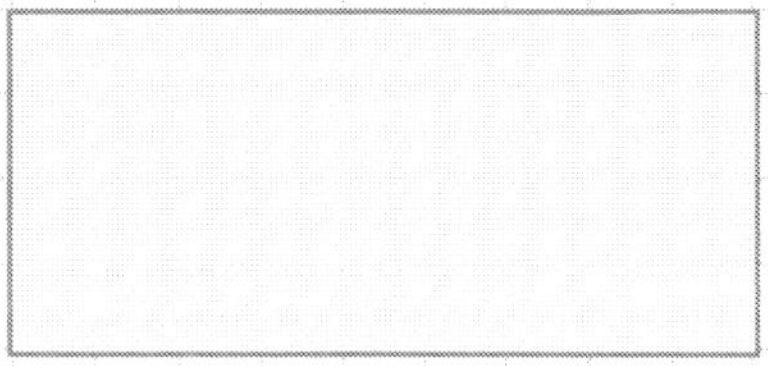

Figure A

Figure B

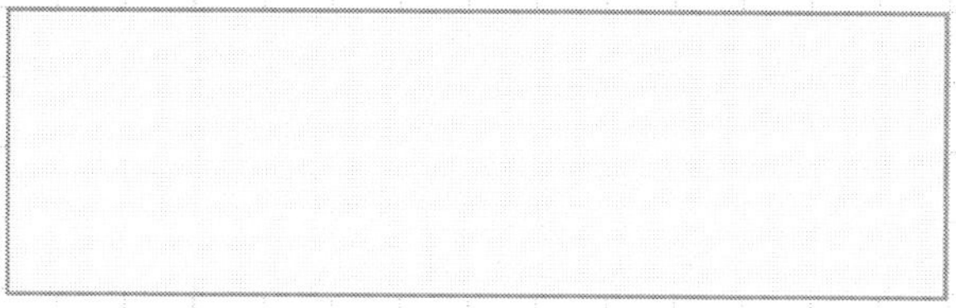

Figure C

4. Which figure is the longest?

A. Figure A

B. Figure B

C. Figure C

SHOW YOUR WORK

5. Which figure is the shortest?

A. Figure A

B. Figure B

C. Figure C

SHOW YOUR WORK

6. How much longer is Figure A than Figure B?

_____ in

SHOW YOUR WORK

7. How much longer is Figure C than Figure B?

_____ in

SHOW YOUR WORK

8. How much longer does Figure A need to be in order to be the same size as Figure C?

_____ in

SHOW YOUR WORK

Use a centimeter ruler and the objects below to answer questions 9 - 15.

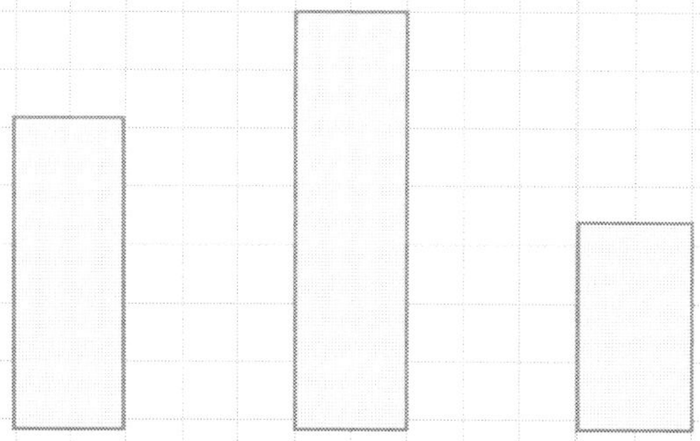

Figure A Figure B Figure C

9. Which figure is the tallest?

A. Figure A

B. Figure B

C. Figure C

SHOW YOUR WORK

10. Which figure is the shortest?

A. Figure A

B. Figure B

C. Figure C

SHOW YOUR WORK

11. How much longer is Figure B than Figure C?

_____ cm

SHOW YOUR WORK

12. How much longer is Figure B than Figure A?

_____ cm

SHOW YOUR WORK

13. How much longer does Figure C need to be in order to be the same size as Figure A?

_____ cm

SHOW YOUR WORK

14. Sarah built a fence that was **5** yards long. Tanya built a fence that was **2** yards longer than Sarah's fence. How long is Tanya's fence?

SHOW YOUR WORK

15. Lara built a tower that was 13 feet tall. Albert built a tower that was **3** feet shorter than Lara's tower. How tall was Albert's tower?

SHOW YOUR WORK

ARGOPREP

3.2.A | Using Addition and Subtraction to Solve Word Problems

We can use addition and subtraction to compare different lengths.

For example:

Joanne's tower is 23 inches tall. Jennifer's tower is 16 inches tall. How much taller is Joanne's tower than Jennifer's tower?

Step 1: Write an equation

We want to find the height **difference** between the two towers. So, we know this is a subtraction problem.

$$23 - 16 = \_\_\_\_\_$$

Step 2: Draw a picture

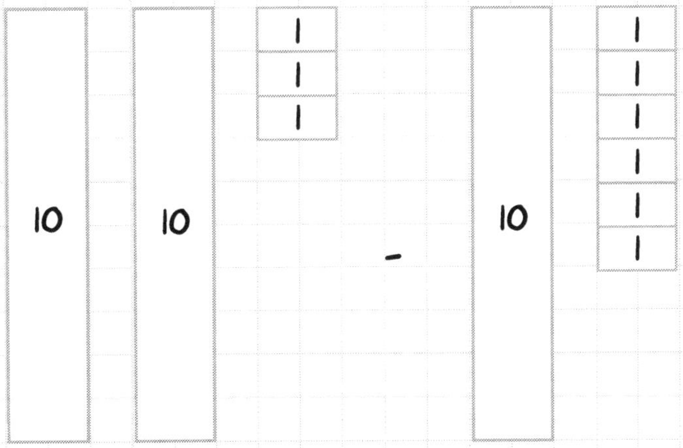

Step 3: Solve

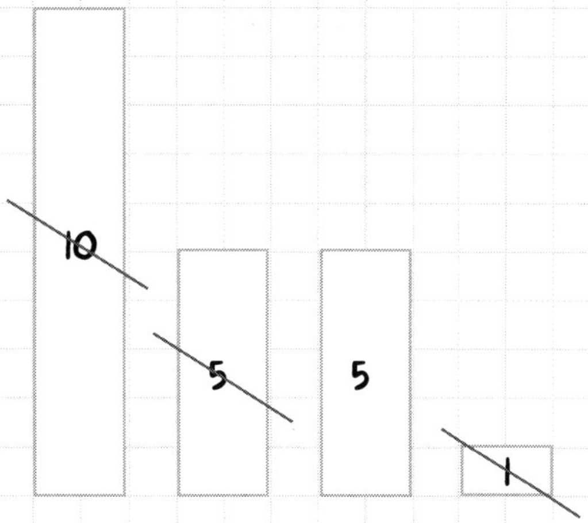

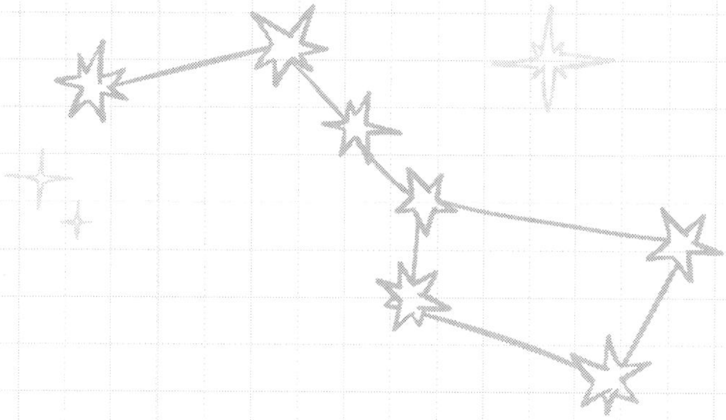

23 - 16 = 7 ✓

ARGOPREP

3.2.A Using Addition and Subtraction to Solve Word Problems

Practice Questions

1. Sloane has two ribbons. One ribbon is **22** cm long. The other ribbon is **36** cm long. What is the length of both ribbons combined? Write and equation to solve the problem.

SHOW YOUR WORK

2. Liam swims **50** meters on Monday, **25** meters on Tuesday and **25** meters on Wednesday. How many meters does he swim in all? Write and equation to solve the problem.

SHOW YOUR WORK

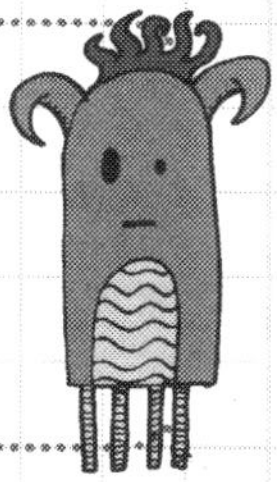

3. Emma runs **45** yards. Her sister runs **55** yards. How many yards do they run altogether? Write and equation to solve the problem.

SHOW YOUR WORK

3.2.A Using Addition and Subtraction to Solve Word Problems

4. Oliver bikes **76** yards in the morning. He bikes another **14** yards after lunch. How far did Oliver bike combined? Write and equation to solve the problem.

SHOW YOUR WORK

5. Charlotte builds a block tower that is **42** centimeters tall. Her friend builds a tower that is **46** centimeters tall. How tall are the towers combined? Write and equation to solve the problem.

SHOW YOUR WORK

6. Hugo is picking flowers. He picks a sunflower that is **60** cm tall. He also picks a tulip that is **34** cm tall. What is the difference in height of the two flowers? Write and equation to solve the problem.

SHOW YOUR WORK

7. Maria purchases two rugs. The red rug is **63** inches long. The blue rug is **26** inches long. How much longer is the red rug than the blue rug? Write and equation to solve the problem.

SHOW YOUR WORK

8. Hiro lives **85** meters from school. Sandra lives **63** meters from school. How much farther does Hiro live from school than Sandra? Write and equation to solve the problem.

SHOW YOUR WORK

9. It snows **72** centimeters in Noah's neighborhood, but it only snows **54** centimeters in Francesco's neighborhood. How much more snow did Noah's neighborhood have compared to Francesco's neighborhood? Write and equation to solve the problem.

SHOW YOUR WORK

ARGOPREP

3.2.A Using Addition and Subtraction to Solve Word Problems

10. Jose is visiting the zoo. He sees one snake that is 45 inches long. He sees another snake that is 32 inches long. What is the difference in length of the two snakes? Write and equation to solve the problem.

SHOW YOUR WORK

Use the chart below to answer questions 11 - 15.

City	Rainfall
Austin	34 in
Seattle	37 in
Buffalo	41 in
Atlanta	49 in
Memphis	54 in
New Orleans	62 in

11. How much more did it rain in Atlanta than in Austin? Write and equation to solve the problem.

SHOW YOUR WORK

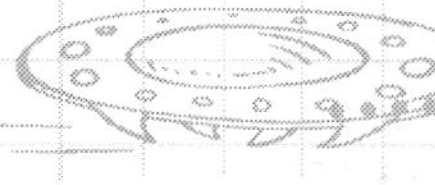

3.2.A Using Addition and Subtraction to Solve Word Problems

12. What was the total rainfall for Austin and Seattle combined? Write an equation to solve the problem.

SHOW YOUR WORK

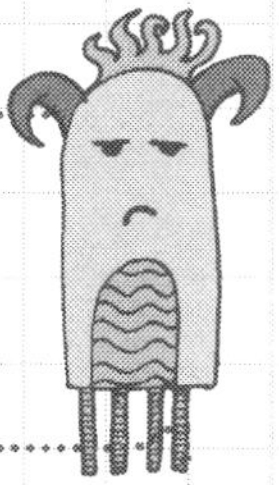

13. How much more did it rain in Memphis than in Seattle? Write an equation to solve the problem.

SHOW YOUR WORK

14. What is the difference in rainfall between the city that received the most rain and the city that received the least rain? Write an equation to solve the problem.

SHOW YOUR WORK

15. What is the total amount of rainfall for the city that received the most rain and the city that received the least rain combined? Write an equation to solve the problem.

SHOW YOUR WORK

3.2.B | Using Addition and Subtraction to Solve Word Problems

Using Number Lines to Solve Word Problems

You can use number lines to help you solve multi-step word problems. Consider the problem below.

There are **85** adults at the party. **4** of the adults leave before dinner is served. Another **2** leave during dinner and **3** leave after dinner. How many adults are left at the party for dessert?

Step One: Draw
The first thing you need to do is set up your number line.

We can tell that this is a subtraction problem because the adults are **leaving** the party. So, we know that our number line can end at **85**. Let's start with **10** hashmarks going backwards.

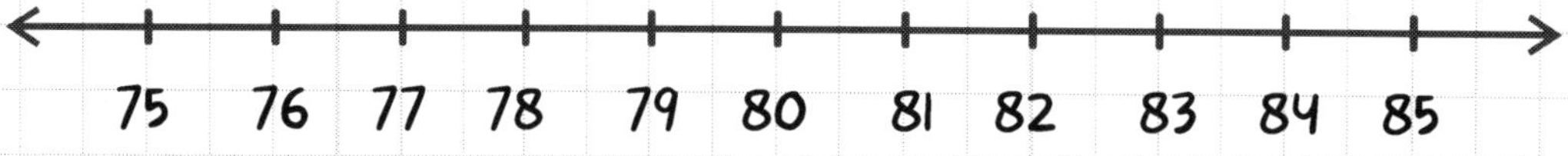

Step Two: Hop
The next step is to use the number line to solve the problem. We do this by moving forward or backward on the number line.

We know we need to hop backward for this problem because we are subtracting. We can determine the number of spaces we need to move by reading the problem.

3.2.B Using Addition and Subtraction to Solve Word Problems

There are **85** adults at the party. 4 of the adults leave before dinner is served. Another 2 leave during dinner and **3** leave after dinner. How many adults are left at the party for dessert?

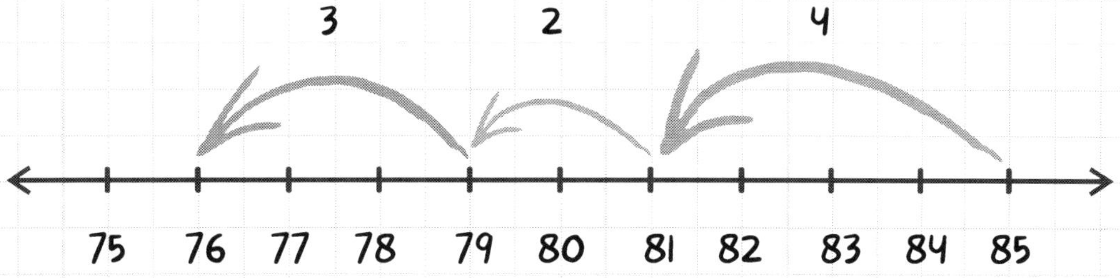

The answer is 76

NOTES

Practice Problems

1. There are **10** birds sitting in a tree. **2** squirrels join them in the tree. **3** rabbits and **1** frog also climb into the tree. How many animals are in the tree? Which number line shows how to solve the problem?

A.

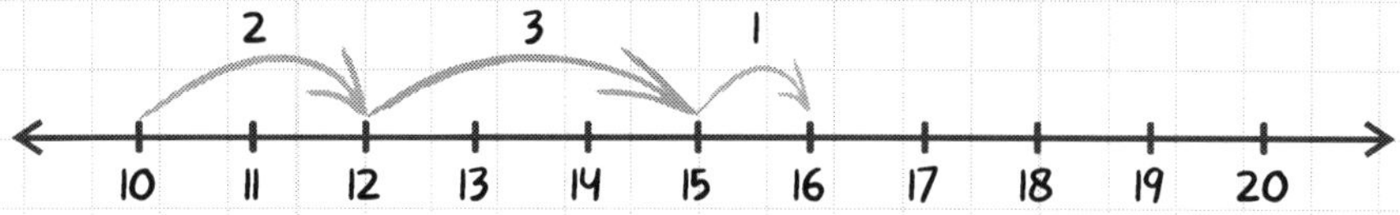

B.

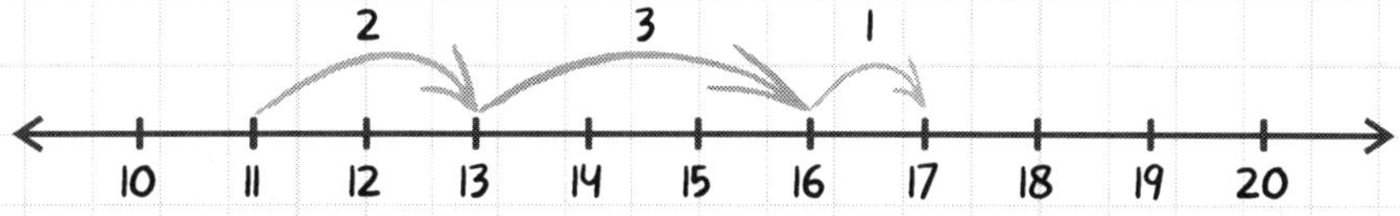

SHOW YOUR WORK

2. There are **30** students in Ms. Pilgrim's class. **3** new students join the class in February. **2** new students join the class in March and **4** new students join the class in May. How many students are in Ms. Pilgrim's class at the end of May? Which number line shows how to solve the problem?

A.

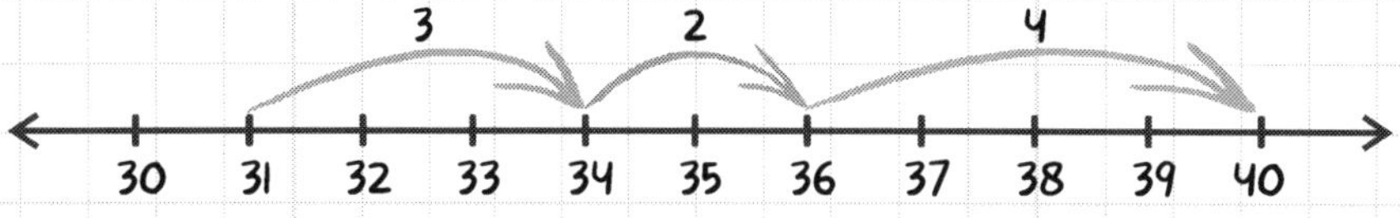

B.

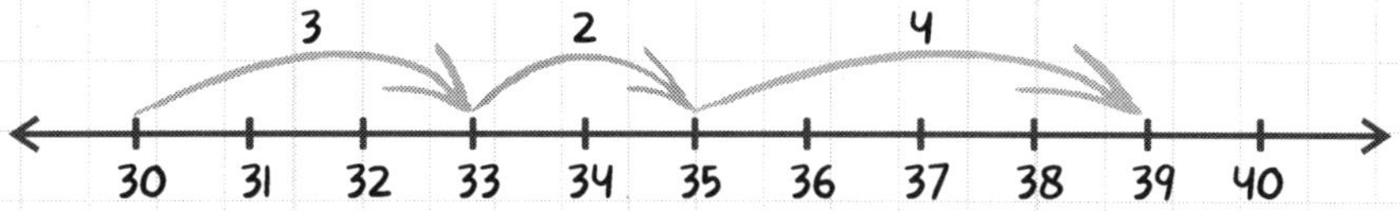

SHOW YOUR WORK

3. There are **80** kids at the party. **3** more kids join the party at snack time, **3** more kids join the party after snack and **2** more kids join the party at lunch time. How many kids are at the party after lunch? Which number line shows how to solve the problem?

A.

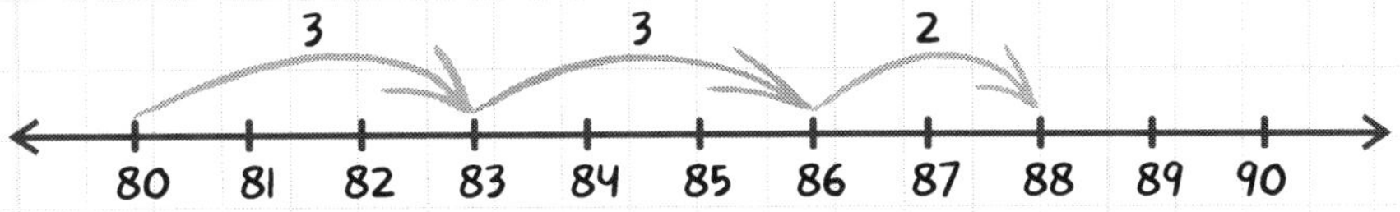

B.

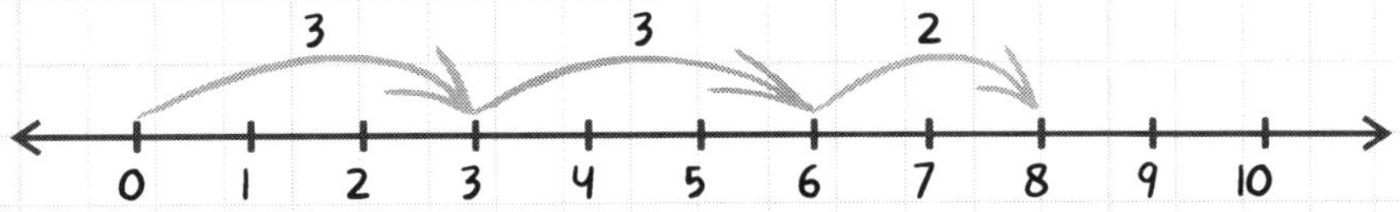

SHOW YOUR WORK

4. Kyle builds a tower of **10** blocks. Sarah adds **2** blocks to the tower. Lara adds **3** blocks to the tower and Fran adds **1** block to the tower. How many blocks does the tower have in all? Which number line shows how to solve the problem below?

A.

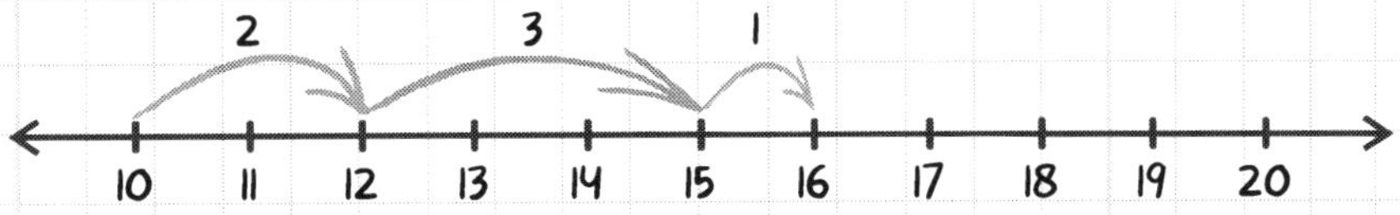

B.

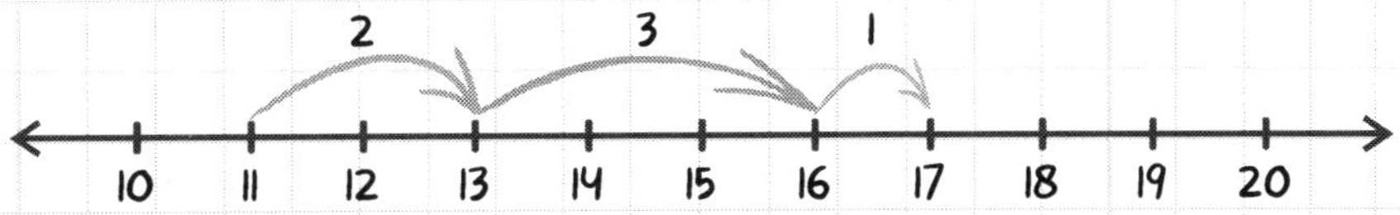

SHOW YOUR WORK

5. The baker makes **3** carrot cupcakes, **3** chocolate cupcakes and **2** vanilla cupcakes. How many cupcakes does she make in all? Which number line shows how to solve the problem?

A.

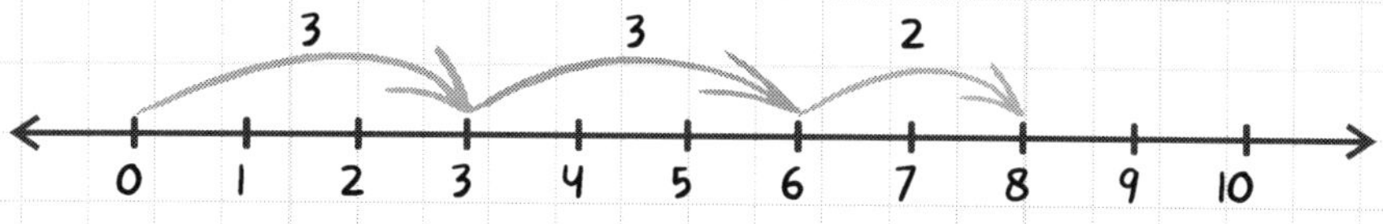

B.

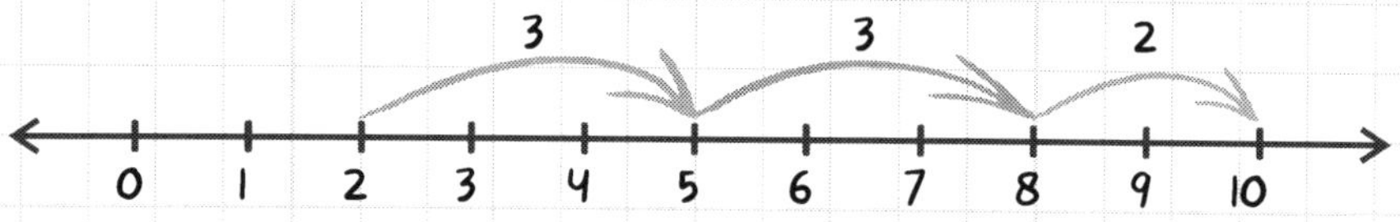

SHOW YOUR WORK

6. There are **38** students in the cafeteria. **2** students leave to use the bathroom, **1** student leaves to see the school nurse and **3** students leave for early dismissal. How many students are left in the cafeteria? Use the number line to solve the problem.

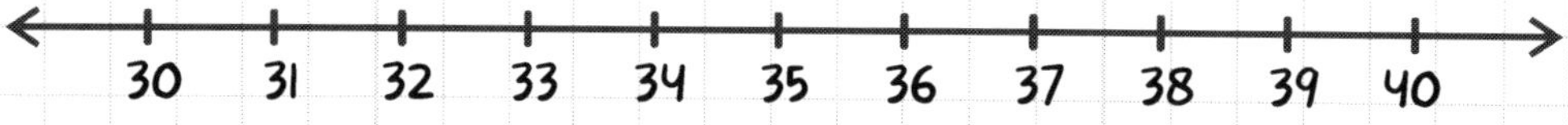

SHOW YOUR WORK

ARGOPREP

3.2.B | Using Addition and Subtraction to Solve Word Problems

7. The chef makes **85** sandwiches. The first grade teachers eat **4** of the sandwiches. The second grade teachers eat **5** of the sandwiches. How many sandwiches are left? Use the number line to solve the problem.

75 76 77 78 79 80 81 82 83 84 85

SHOW YOUR WORK

8. Alex had **18** pencils. He gave **2** pencils to his best friend and **4** pencils to his sister. How many pencils does he have left? Use the number line to solve the problem.

10 11 12 13 14 15 16 17 18 19 20

SHOW YOUR WORK

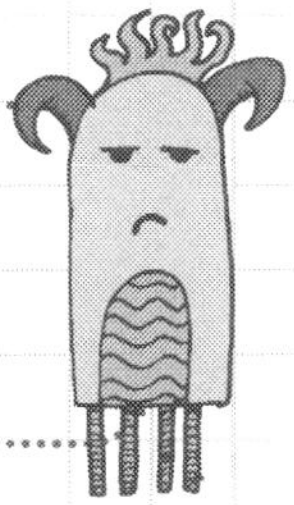

9. The squirrel collected **90** nuts for winter. It drops **6** nuts on its way to the tree. It drops another **3** nuts while climbing up the tree. How many nuts does the squirrel have left? Use the number line to solve the problem.

80 81 82 83 84 85 86 87 88 89 90

SHOW YOUR WORK

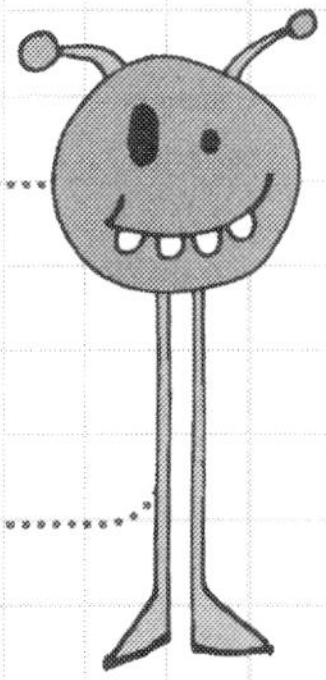

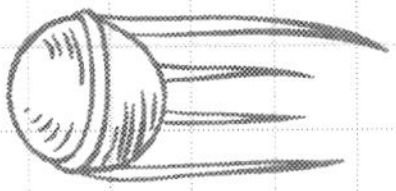

3.2.B Using Addition and Subtraction to Solve Word Problems

10. Sofia has **40** cupcakes for her class. She gives **4** to her friends and **5** to her siblings. How many cupcakes does she have left for her classmates? Use the number line to solve the problem.

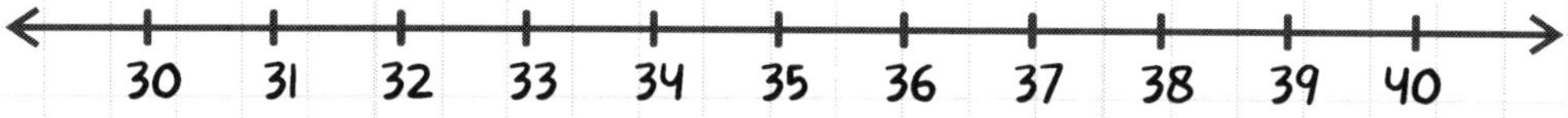

SHOW YOUR WORK

11. There were **26** people on a rollercoaster. **9** got off the ride. How many people are still on the rollercoaster? Create a number line to solve the problem.

SHOW YOUR WORK

12. There are **35** students in the gym. **7** students join them after recess. How many students are in the gym now? Create a number line to solve the problem.

SHOW YOUR WORK

ARGOPREP

3.2.B | Using Addition and Subtraction to Solve Word Problems

13. Sarah's family bakes 64 cookies for the party. 12 cookies are eaten before the guests arrive. How many cookies are left for the party? Create a number line to solve the problem.

SHOW YOUR WORK

14. Leo read 47 books over summer break. He read another 4 books over fall break and another 5 books over winter break. How many books did he read during the three breaks combined? Create a number line to solve the problem.

SHOW YOUR WORK

15. 70 birds are in a tree. 11 fly away when a truck honks its horn. Another 4 fly away when it starts to rain. How many birds are left in the tree? Create a number line to solve the problem.

SHOW YOUR WORK

3.3.A | Working with Time and Money

We use analog and digital clocks to tell time.

Analog Clock

Analog clocks use hour and minute marks to display the time. Each hour mark is labeled with a number. There are **5** minute marks in between each hour mark.

Digital Clock

A digital clock uses numbers to display time. The hour is displayed to the left of the colon. The minutes are displayed to the right of the colon.

Let's look at an example.

What time is it?

Step 1: Read the hour hand

The hour hand is pointing slightly after the **2**, which means it's between **2** and **3** o'clock.

Step 2: Read the minute hand

The minute hand is pointing at the 1. We know that there are **5** minutes between each hour mark. So, it must be **2:05**.

The time is **2:05** ✓

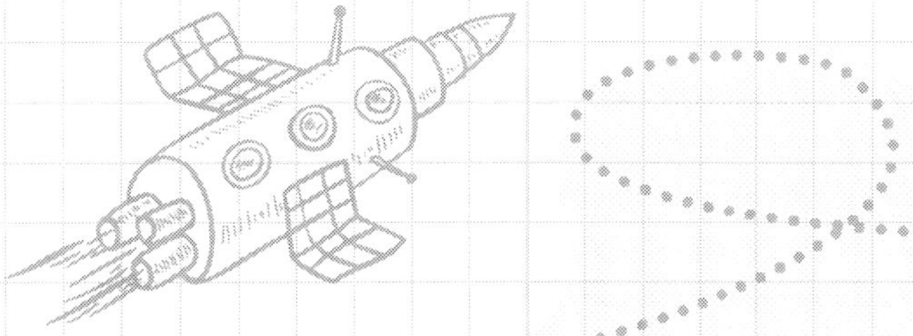

Practice Questions

1. Write the time shown on the clock below.

SHOW YOUR WORK

2. Write the time shown on the clock below.

SHOW YOUR WORK

3. Write the time shown on the clock below.

SHOW YOUR WORK

4. Write the time shown on the clock below.

SHOW YOUR WORK

5. Write the time shown on the clock below.

SHOW YOUR WORK

6. Which clock shows 1:15?

A.

B.

SHOW YOUR WORK

7. Which clock shows 3:25?

A.

B.

SHOW YOUR WORK

8. Which clock shows 2:10?

A.

B.

SHOW YOUR WORK

9. Which clock shows 7:45?

A.

B.

SHOW YOUR WORK

10. Which clock shows 3:05?

A.

B.

SHOW YOUR WORK

11. Which clock shows 4:20?

A.

B.

SHOW YOUR WORK

12. Draw the hands on the clock to show 1:30

SHOW YOUR WORK

13. Draw the hands on the clock to show 5:45

SHOW YOUR WORK

14. Draw the hands on the clock to show **2:55**

SHOW YOUR WORK

15. Draw the hands on the clock to show **4:45**

SHOW YOUR WORK

NOTES

Working with Money

We can use what we know about money to solve word problems involving dollars and coins.

In first grade, we learned the value of each coin.

penny	nickel	dime	quarter
1	5	10	25

Consider the problem below.

Show two ways to make **36¢** using pennies, nickels, dimes and quarters.

10 + 10 + 10 + 5 + 1 = 36

OR

25 + 10 + 1 = 36

Practice Problems

1. Show two ways to make **26¢** using pennies, nickels, dimes and quarters.

SHOW YOUR WORK

2. Show two ways to make **51¢** using pennies, nickels, dimes and quarters.

SHOW YOUR WORK

3. Show two ways to make **37¢** using pennies, nickels, dimes and quarters.

SHOW YOUR WORK

4. Show two ways to make **16¢** using pennies, nickels, dimes and quarters.

SHOW YOUR WORK

5. Show two ways to make **83¢** using pennies, nickels, dimes and quarters.

SHOW YOUR WORK

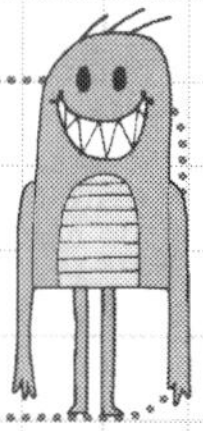

6. Peter has **3** one dollar bills, **2** five dollar bills and **3** ten dollar bills. How much money does he have in all?

SHOW YOUR WORK

3.3.B | Working with Time and Money

7. Jasmine has **2** one dollar bills and **3** five dollar bills.
How much money does she have in all?

SHOW YOUR WORK

8. Carter has **7** one dollar bills, **1** five dollar bill and **5** ten dollar bills. How much money does he have in all?

SHOW YOUR WORK

9. Jake has **5** five dollar bills and **2** ten dollar bills.
How much money does he have in all?

SHOW YOUR WORK

10. Gus has **5** one dollar bills, **5** five dollar bills and **3** ten dollar bills.
How much money does he have in all?

SHOW YOUR WORK

Working with Time and Money

11. What is the total value of the coins below?

SHOW YOUR WORK

12. What is the total value of the coins below?

SHOW YOUR WORK

13. What is the total value of the coins below?

SHOW YOUR WORK

14. What is the total value of the coins below?

SHOW YOUR WORK

15. What is the total value of the coins below?

SHOW YOUR WORK

NOTES

We can use line plots to better understand data we've collected. Let's look at an example.

Srinivas measured seven different block towers. The heights were 7, 9, 9, 14, 17, 17 and 20 inches. Create a line plot of the heights.

Step 1: Draw a Number Line

We need to create a number line in order to plot each point. The number line should include all of the numbers in our data set. Since the numbers in our data set range from 7 to 20, we will draw a number line from 5 - 20. We will add a label at the bottom of the number line to show that the numbers represent inches.

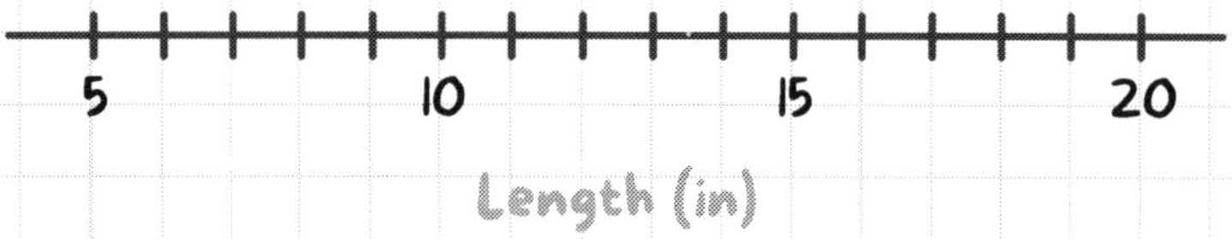

Step 2: Plot Each Point

The next step is to plot each point. We do this by drawing a dot for each number in our data set. The dots go above each number on the number line.

Our data set includes: 7, 9, 9, 14, 17, 17, and 20

Some of these numbers appear more than once. Add a dot for each time the number appears in the data set.

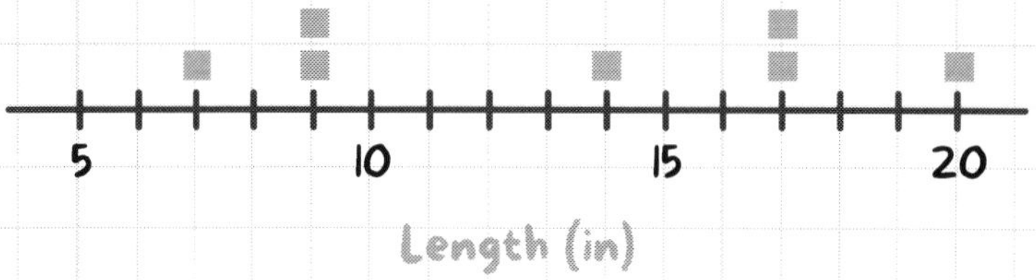

The line plot helps us see the different heights more quickly and clearly.

3.4.A | Represent Data

Practice Questions

1. Kate measured her flowers. The lengths were 11, 14, 14, 17 and 20 inches. Create a line plot of the lengths.

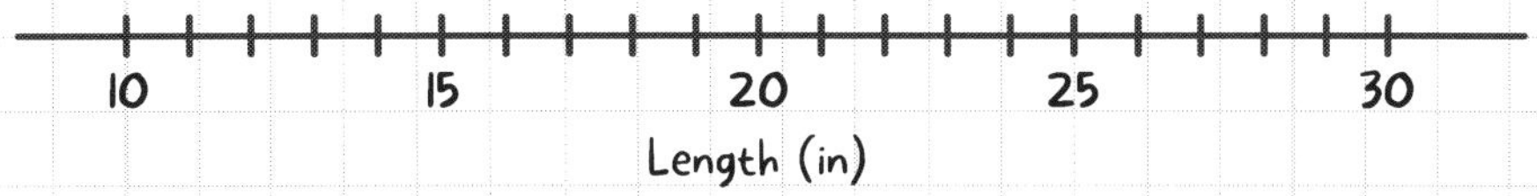

SHOW YOUR WORK

2. Baylee measured her batons. The lengths were 12, 15, 15, 18 and 25 inches. Create a line plot of the lengths.

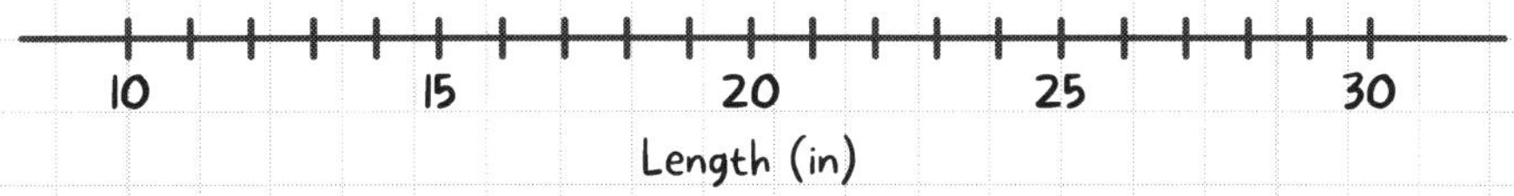

SHOW YOUR WORK

3. Sam measured five toy boats. The lengths were 25, 25, 29, 31 and 31 inches. Create a line plot of the lengths.

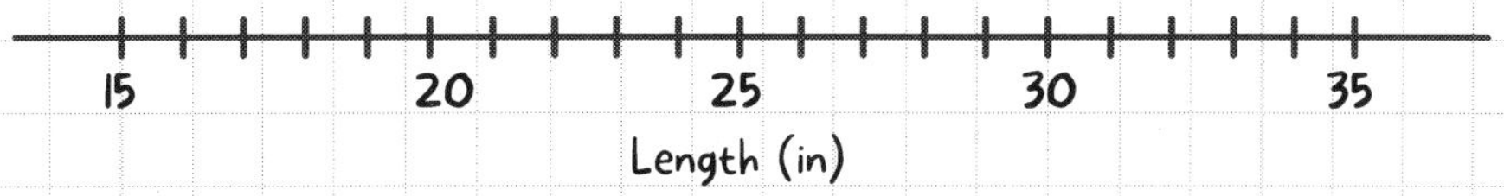

SHOW YOUR WORK

3.4.A | Represent Data

4. Mary measured five pine trees. The heights were **26, 26, 28, 30** and **32** feet. Create a line plot of the lengths.

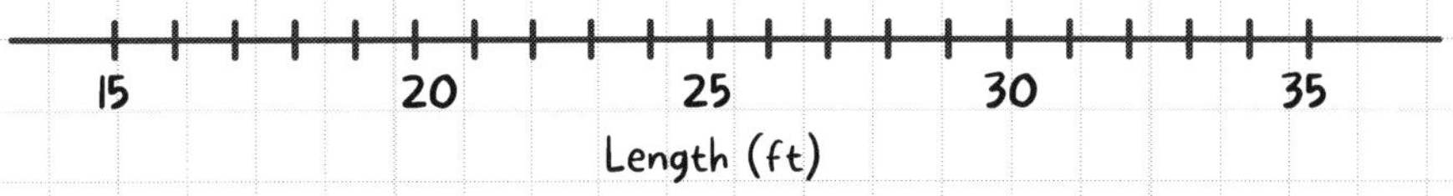

SHOW YOUR WORK

5. Octavia measured five of her books. The lengths were **7, 10, 15, 20** and **20** inches. Create a line plot of the lengths.

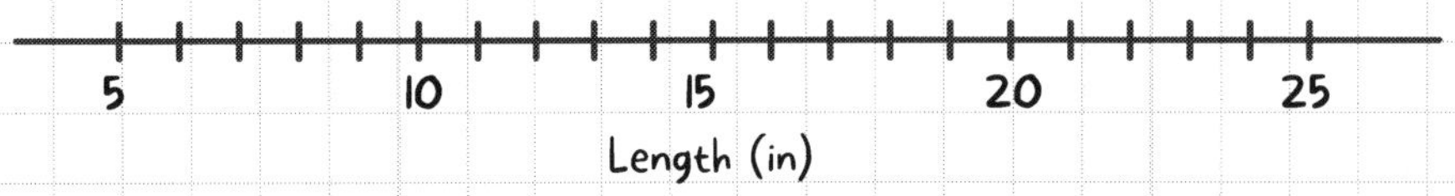

SHOW YOUR WORK

3.4.A | Represent Data

6. Create a line plot for the data below.

Fruit	Length
Apple	3 in
Banana	5 in
Grape	2 in
Strawberry	2 in

SHOW YOUR WORK

7. Create a line plot for the data below.

Flower	Height in Inches
Rose	7 in
Tulip	5 in
Sunflower	12 in
Daisy	5 in

SHOW YOUR WORK

3.4.A | Represent Data

8. Create a line plot for the data below.

City	Amount of Snow
Chicago	10 in
New York	6 in
Buffalo	12 in
Toronto	10 in

SHOW YOUR WORK

9. Create a line plot for the data below.

City	Amount of Rain
Chicago	8 in
New York	8 in
Buffalo	10 in
Toronto	5 in

SHOW YOUR WORK

10. Create a line plot for the data below.

Tower	Height
Tower A	3 ft
Tower B	5 ft
Tower C	4 ft
Tower D	4 ft

SHOW YOUR WORK

3.4.A | Represent Data

Use the chart to answer questions 11 - 15

Tower	Height
Tower A	6 ft
Tower B	5 ft
Tower C	9 ft
Tower D	6 ft
Tower E	10 ft
Tower F	5 ft
Tower G	5 ft

11. How many plot points will represent 5 ft?

A. 1

B. 2

C. 3

D. 4

SHOW YOUR WORK

12. How many plot points will represent 6 ft?

A. 1

B. 2

C. 3

D. 4

SHOW YOUR WORK

13. How many plot points will represent 9 ft?

A. 1

B. 2

C. 3

D. 4

SHOW YOUR WORK

14. How many plot points will represent 10 ft?

A. 1

B. 2

C. 3

D. 4

SHOW YOUR WORK

15. Create a line plot for the data.

SHOW YOUR WORK

3.4.B | Represent Data

Interpret Data

Picture graphs and **bar graphs** can also help us visualize data.

Let's create a picture graph for the data set below.

Student	Ice Cream Cones
Sarah	3
BJ	5
Zofia	2

A **picture graph** uses pictures instead of dots. For this problem, we will use ice cream cones. According to the chart, BJ had 5 ice cream cones, Sarah had 3 and Zofia had 2.

Our picture graph will look like this:

3.4.B | Represent Data

What about a bar graph?

Instead of pictures, a bar graph uses simple bars to display data. Lets try it with our example problem.

Student	Ice Cream Cones
Sarah	3
BJ	5
Zofia	2

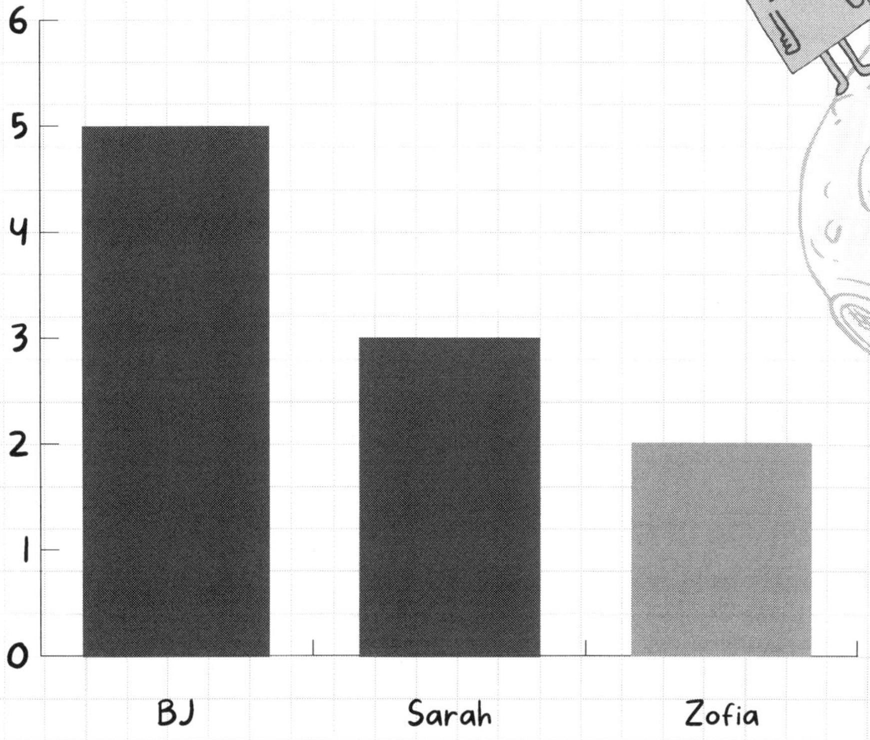

3.4.B | Represent Data

Practice Questions

Use the bar graph to answer questions 1 - 5.

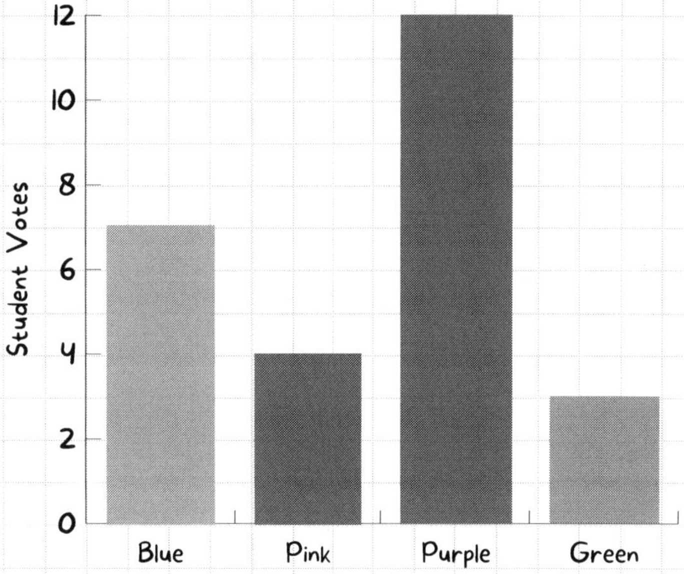

1. ________ had more votes than blue.

A. Pink

B. Purple

C. Green

SHOW YOUR WORK

2. ________ had the most votes.

A. Pink

B. Purple

C. Green

SHOW YOUR WORK

3.4.B | Represent Data

3. _________ had the least votes.

A. Pink

B. Purple

C. Green

SHOW YOUR WORK

4. How many students voted for pink and purple combined?

SHOW YOUR WORK

5. How many more students voted for purple than green?

SHOW YOUR WORK

3.4.B | Represent Data

Use the chart to answer questions 6 - 10.

Flavor	Student Votes
Chocolate	11
Vanilla	14
Cookie Dough	8

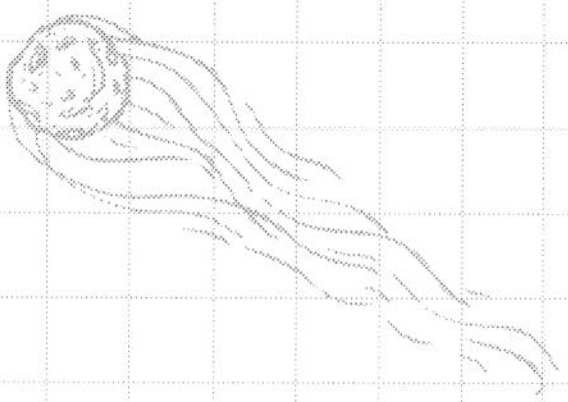

6. Create a bar graph for the data.

SHOW YOUR WORK

7. _________ had the most votes.

A. Chocolate

B. Vanilla

C. Cookie Dough

SHOW YOUR WORK

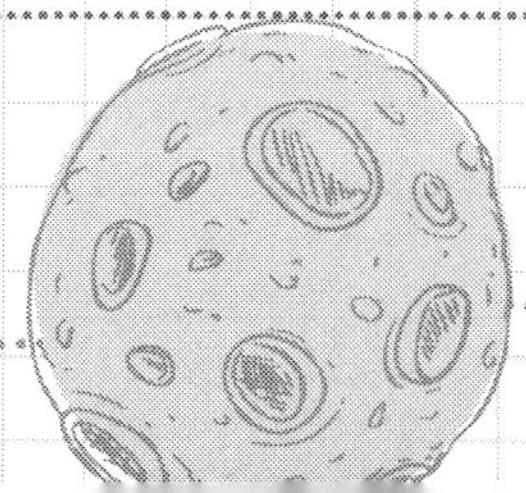

3.4.B Represent Data

8. _________ had the least votes.

A. Chocolate

B. Vanilla

C. Cookie Dough

SHOW YOUR WORK

9. How many people voted for chocolate and vanilla combined?

SHOW YOUR WORK

10. How many more people voted for vanilla than chocolate?

SHOW YOUR WORK

3.4.B | Represent Data

Use the picture graph to answer questions 11 - 15.

Student	Pieces of Pizza
Anna	3
Betty	5
Chris	1

11. Create a picture graph for the data.

SHOW YOUR WORK

12. _________ ate the most pizza.

A. Anna

B. Betty

C. Chris

SHOW YOUR WORK

13. _________ ate the least pizza.

A. Anna

B. Betty

C. Chris

SHOW YOUR WORK

14. How many more pieces of pizza did Betty eat than Chris?

SHOW YOUR WORK

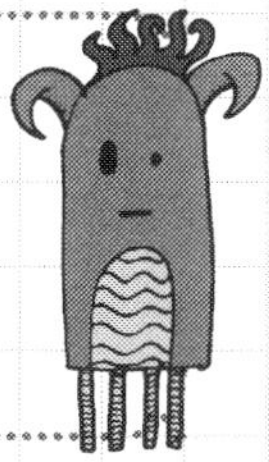

15. How many pieces of pizza did the students eat all together?

SHOW YOUR WORK

3.5 | Chapter Test

Use a ruler for questions 1 - 4

1. What is the length of the caterpillar?

________ cm

SHOW YOUR WORK

2. What is the height of the caterpillar?

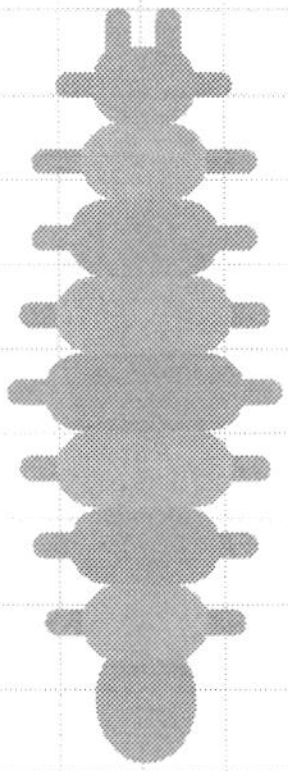

________ cm

SHOW YOUR WORK

3. What is the length of the caterpillar?

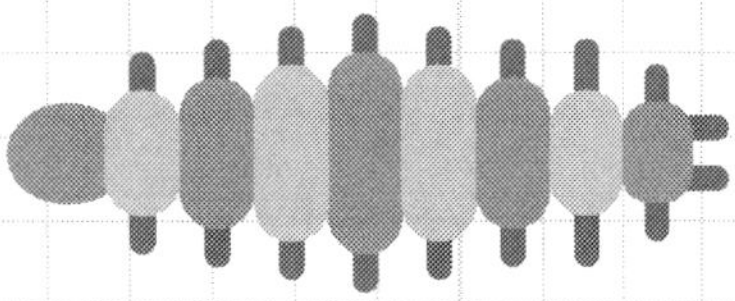

________ in

SHOW YOUR WORK

4. What is the height of the caterpillar?

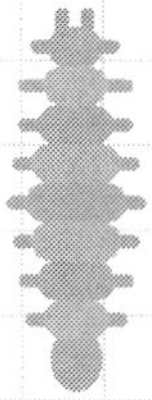

________ in

SHOW YOUR WORK

3.5 Chapter Test

Use the conversion chart to answer questions **5 - 6**

Conversion Chart
1 feet = 12 inches
1 yard = 3 feet
1 meter = 100 cm

5. The field is **5** yards. How many feet is the field?

SHOW YOUR WORK

6. The garden is **3** feet long. What is the length in inches?

SHOW YOUR WORK

7. Lauren has two ribbons. One ribbon is **12** cm long. The other ribbon is **26** cm long. What is the length of both ribbons combined? Write an equation to solve the problem.

SHOW YOUR WORK

8. There are **32** students in Ms. Plum's class. **3** move away before winter break. Two more move away during spring break. How many students are left in Ms. Plum's class after spring break? Use a number line to solve the problem

SHOW YOUR WORK

9. There are **11** people at the party. **2** adults arrive at the party late. They bring **3** toddlers and **1** baby with them. How many people are at the party in all? Which number line shows how to solve the problem?

A.

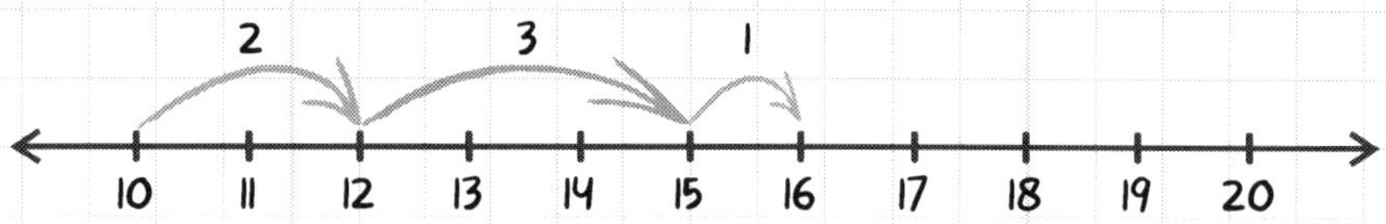

B.

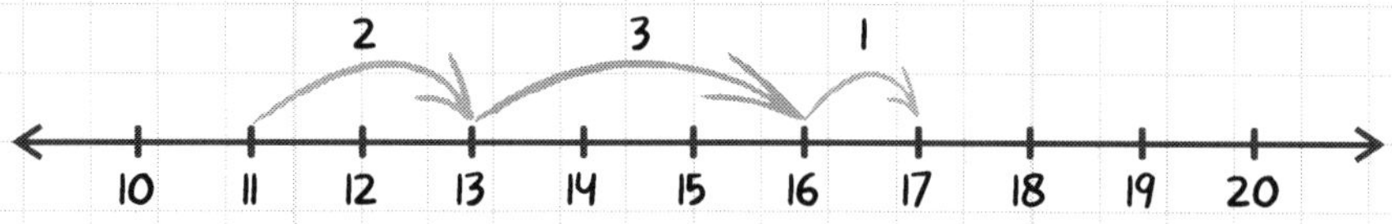

SHOW YOUR WORK

10. Draw the hands on the clock to show **6:15**

SHOW YOUR WORK

11. Write the time shown on the clock below.

SHOW YOUR WORK

9:35

Big hand on the 7 with

12. Lara has **5** one-dollar bills, **1** five-dollar bill and **3** ten-dollar bills. How much money does she have in all?

SHOW YOUR WORK

13. Show two ways to make **75¢** using pennies, nickels, dimes and quarters.

SHOW YOUR WORK

14. About how tall is the flower?

1 cm

SHOW YOUR WORK

3.5 | Chapter Test

15. How much longer is Line A than Line B?

SHOW YOUR WORK

16. Kate measured her flowers. The lengths were 11, 14, 14, 17 and 20 inches. Create a line plot of the lengths.

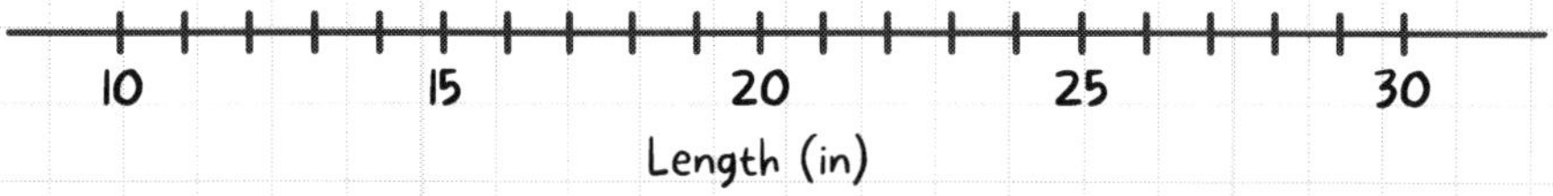

SHOW YOUR WORK

17. Jim measured five sticks. The lengths were 20, 22, 24, 24 and 30 centimeters. Create a line plot of the lengths.

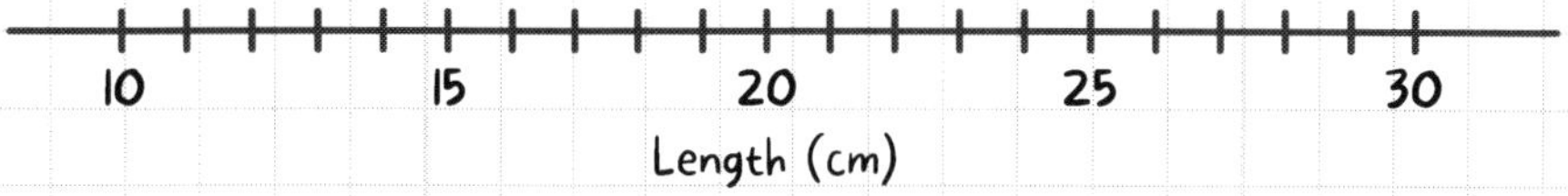

SHOW YOUR WORK

3.5 Chapter Test

Use the chart below to answer questions 18 - 20

Pizza	Student Votes
Pepperoni	6
Cheese	14
Sausage	3

18. Create a bar graph for the data.

SHOW YOUR WORK

19. Which pizza received the most votes?

SHOW YOUR WORK

20. Which pizza received the fewest votes?

SHOW YOUR WORK

Chapter 4:
Geometry

4.1. Recognizing and Drawing Shapes page 200

4.2. Chapter Test page 219

ARGOPREP

ARGOPREP

4.1.A | Recognizing and Drawing Shapes

We can use what we know about geometry to help us identify and draw different shapes. In second grade, we need to be familiar with triangles, quadrilaterals, pentagons and hexagons.

Triangles

A closed shape with **3** straight kl.;/ sides and **3** angles.

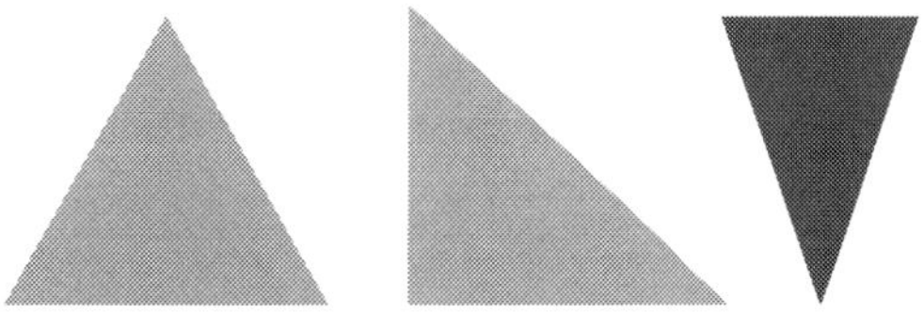

Quadrilaterals

A closed shape with **4** straight sides

Pentagons

A closed figure with **5** straight sides

Hexagons

A closed figure with **6** straight sides

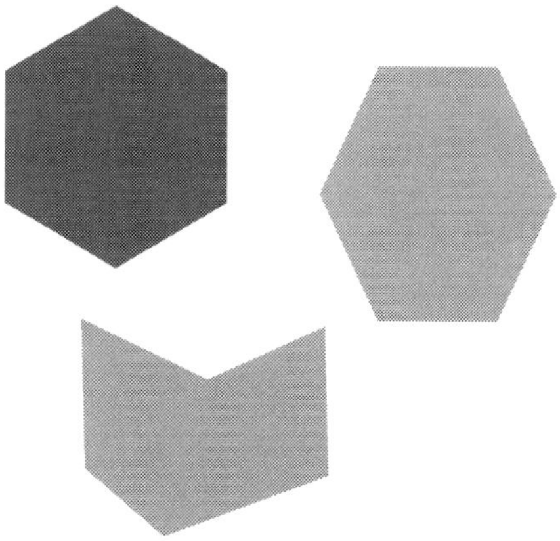

Practice Questions

1. Draw a closed shape that has 4 straight sides. What is the name of the shape?

SHOW YOUR WORK

2. Draw a closed shape with 6 straight sides. What is the name of the shape?

SHOW YOUR WORK

3. Draw a closed shape with 3 straight sides. What is the name of the shape?

SHOW YOUR WORK

4. Draw a closed shape with 5 straight sides. What is the name of the shape?

SHOW YOUR WORK

5. Circle all of the pentagons

A. 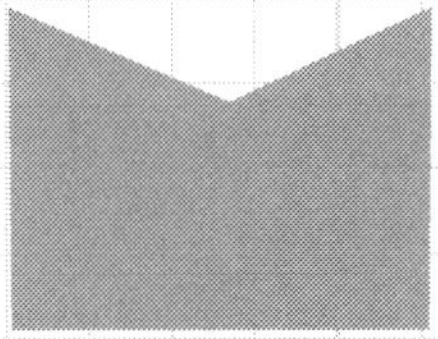

C. 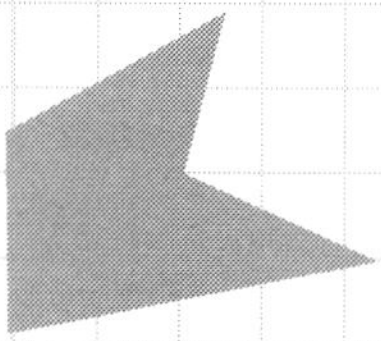

B. 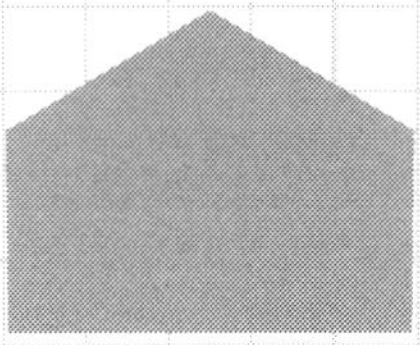

D. 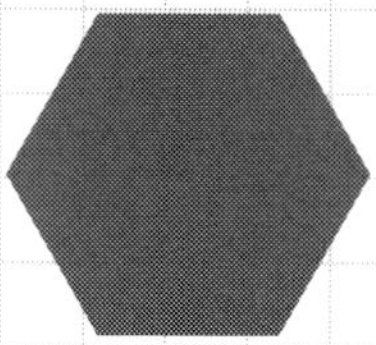

SHOW YOUR WORK

6. Circle all of the triangles

A. 

C. 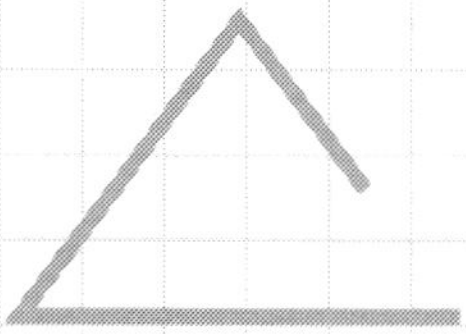

B. 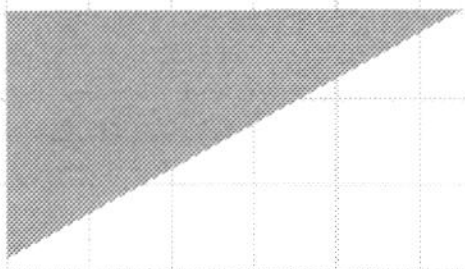

D. 

SHOW YOUR WORK

7. Circle all of the quadrilaterals

A. 

C. 

B. 

D. 

SHOW YOUR WORK

8. Circle all of the hexagons

A. 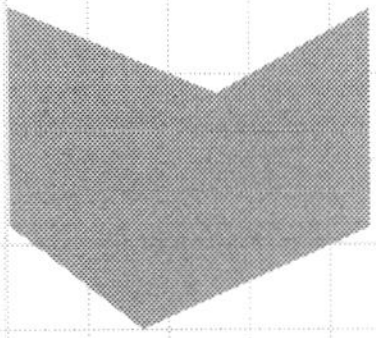

C. 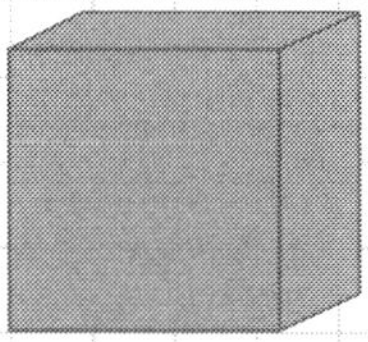

B. 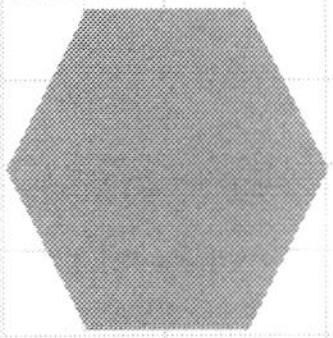

D. 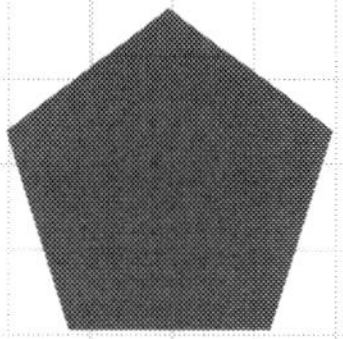

SHOW YOUR WORK

9. I am a closed shape with **5** straight sides. What shape am I?

SHOW YOUR WORK

10. I am a closed shape with **4** straight sides. What shape am I?

SHOW YOUR WORK

11. I am a closed shape with **6** straight sides. What shape am I?

SHOW YOUR WORK

12. Draw two different quadrilaterals.

SHOW YOUR WORK

13. Draw two different triangles.

SHOW YOUR WORK

14. Draw two different pentagons.

SHOW YOUR WORK

15. Draw two different hexagons.

SHOW YOUR WORK

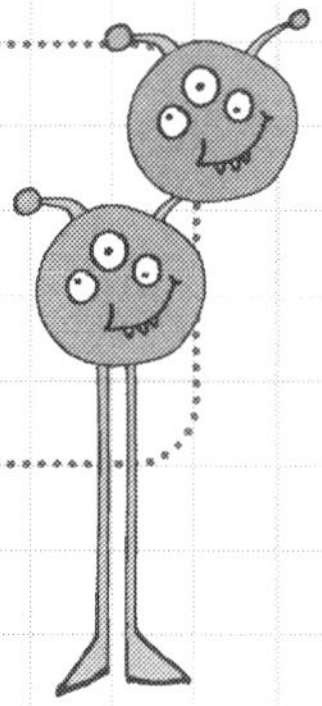

Partitioning Rectangles

PARTITION

Dividing shapes into equal parts..

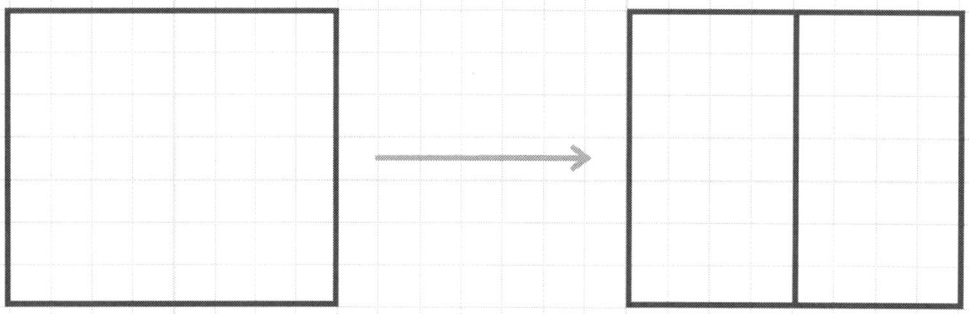

ROWS are horizontal.

They are drawn side to side.

COLUMNS are vertical.

They are drawn up and down.

Partition the rectangle into 4 rows and 2 columns.

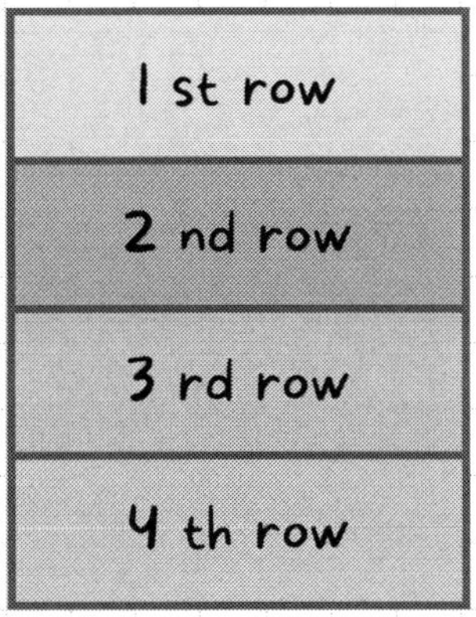

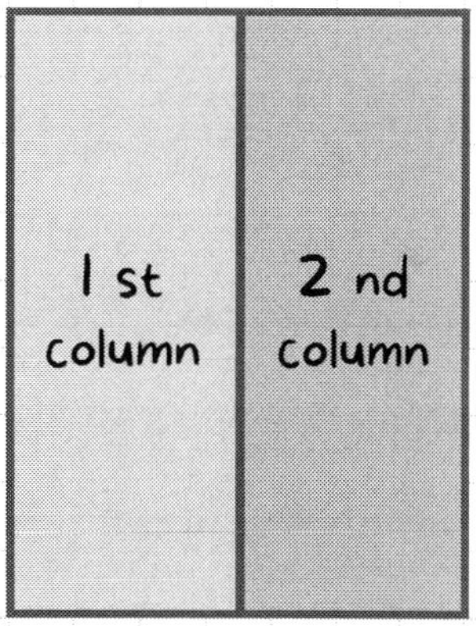

Practice Questions

1. Partition the rectangle into 2 rows and 2 columns.

SHOW YOUR WORK

2. How many squares did you create in all?

SHOW YOUR WORK

3. How many squares are in each column?

SHOW YOUR WORK

4. How many squares are in each row?

SHOW YOUR WORK

5. Partition the rectangle into 4 rows and 3 columns.

SHOW YOUR WORK

6. How many squares did you create in all?

SHOW YOUR WORK

7. How many squares are in each column?

SHOW YOUR WORK

8. How many squares are in each row?

SHOW YOUR WORK

9. Partition the rectangle into **5** rows and **3** columns.

SHOW YOUR WORK

10. How many squares did you create in all?

SHOW YOUR WORK

11. How many squares are in each column?

SHOW YOUR WORK

12. How many squares are in each row?

SHOW YOUR WORK

13. Partition the rectangle into 3 rows and 4 columns.

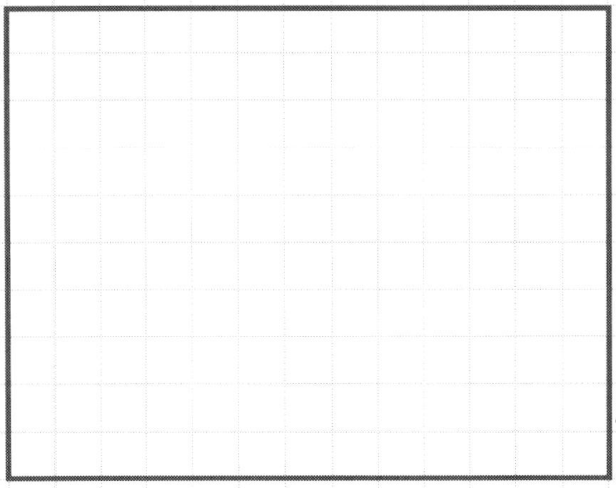

SHOW YOUR WORK

14. How many squares did you create in all?

SHOW YOUR WORK

15. How many squares are in each column?

SHOW YOUR WORK

16. How many squares are in each row?

SHOW YOUR WORK

Partitioning Shapes into Halves, Thirds, and Fourths

We can use what we know about partitioning shapes to divide circles and rectangles into halves, thirds and fourths.

Halves

To partition a shape into halves, divide it into two equal parts. Each part is called one-half.

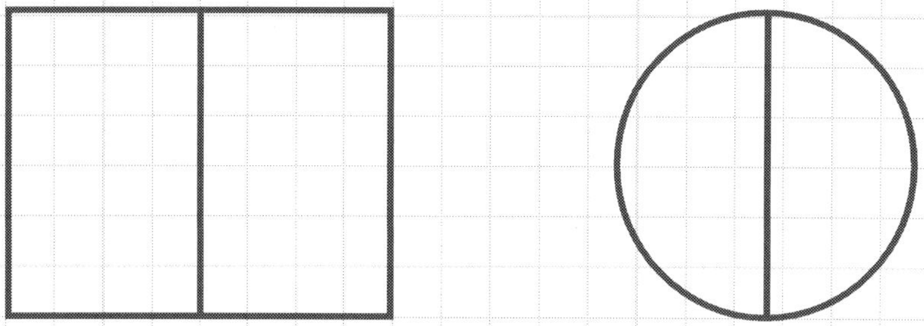

Thirds

To partition a shape into thirds, divide it into three equal parts. Each part is called one-third.

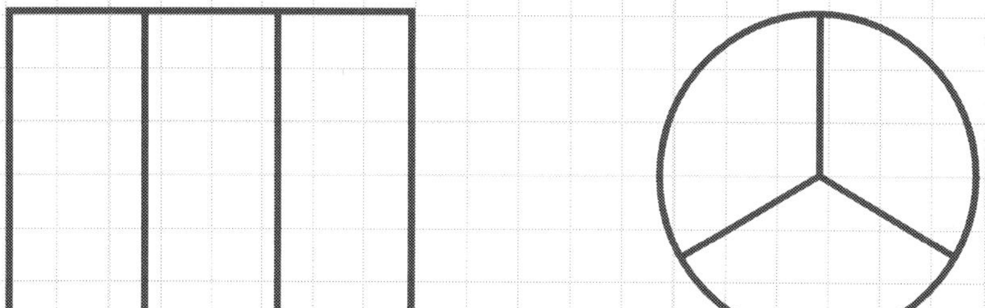

Fourths

To partition a shape into fourths, divide it into four equal parts. Each part is called one-fourth.

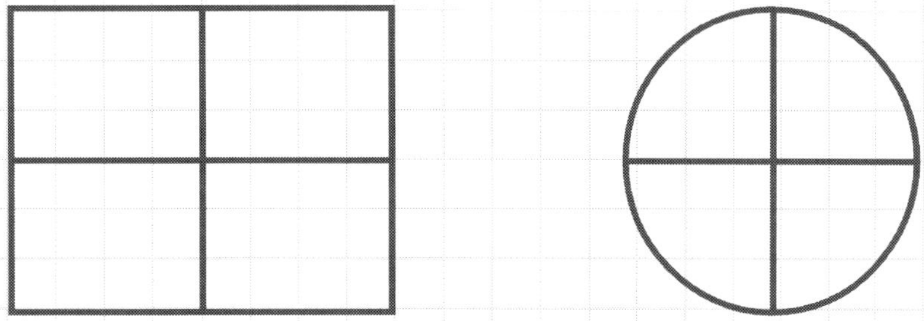

Practice Questions

1. Which rectangle is partitioned into thirds?

A. 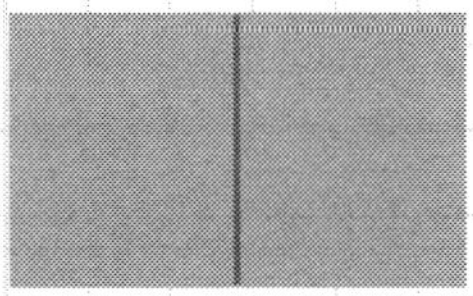

B. 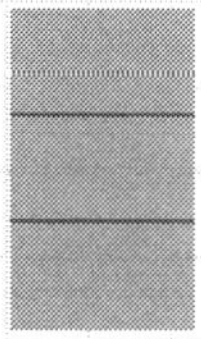

C. 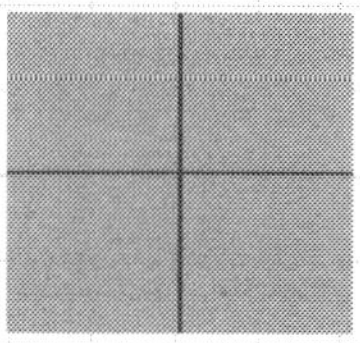

SHOW YOUR WORK

2. Which rectangle is partitioned into fourths?

A. 

B. 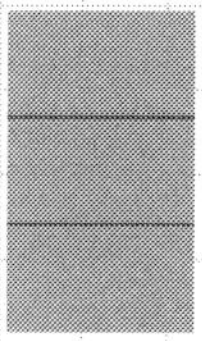

C. 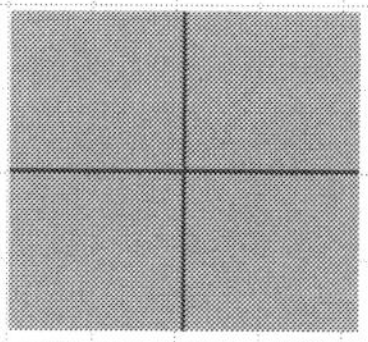

SHOW YOUR WORK

3. Which rectangle is partitioned into halves?

A. 

B. 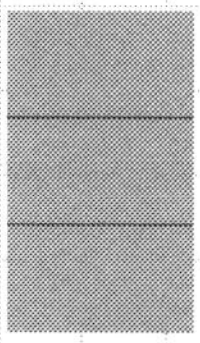

C. 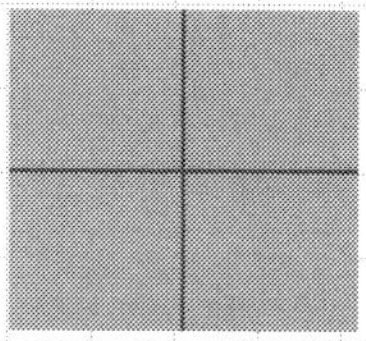

SHOW YOUR WORK

4. Which circle is partitioned into thirds?

A. 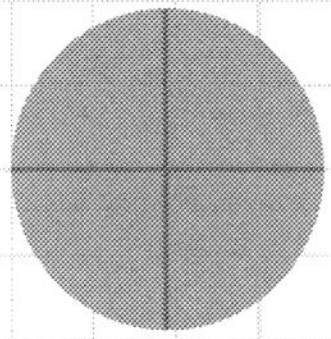

B. 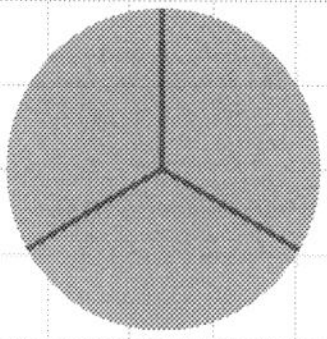

C. 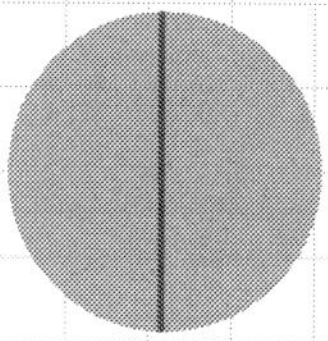

SHOW YOUR WORK

5. Which circle is partitioned into fourths?

A. 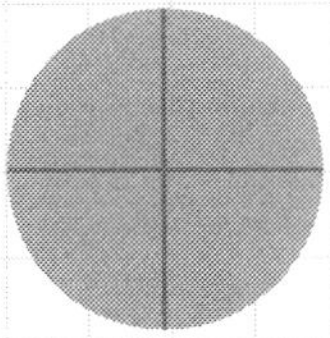

B. 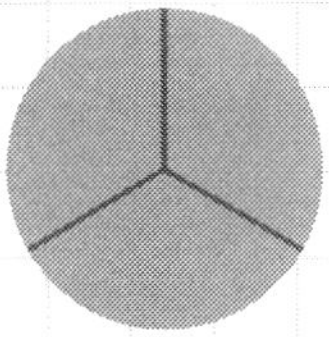

C. 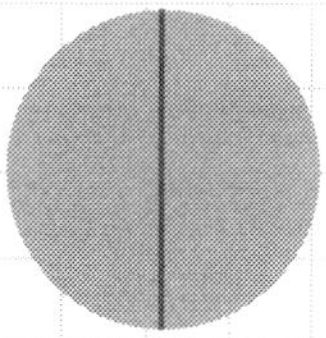

SHOW YOUR WORK

6. Which circle is partitioned into halves?

A. 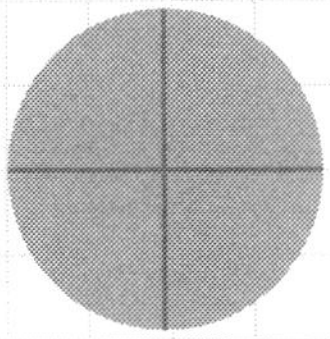

B. 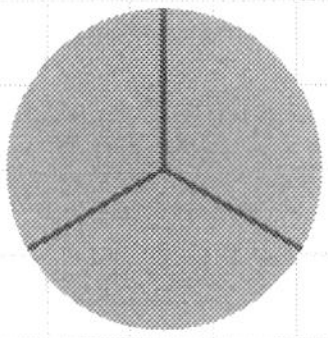

C. 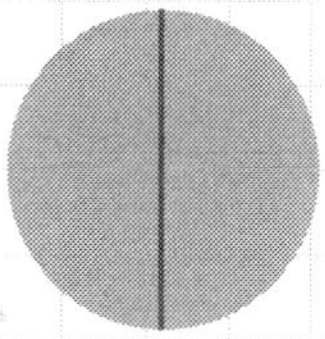

SHOW YOUR WORK

7. Partition the rectangles into halves in different ways.

SHOW YOUR WORK

8. Partition the rectangles into thirds in different ways.

SHOW YOUR WORK

9. Partition the rectangles into fourths in different ways.

SHOW YOUR WORK

10. Each piece of the circle equals _____.

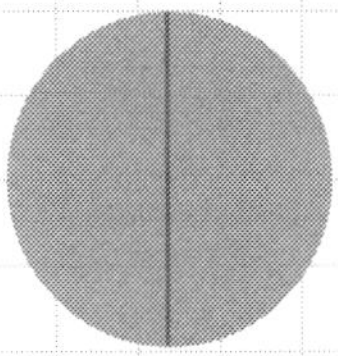

A. one-half

B. one-third

C. one-fourth

SHOW YOUR WORK

11. Each piece of the circle equals _____.

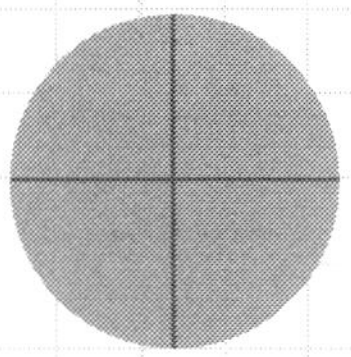

A. one-half

B. one-third

C. one-fourth

SHOW YOUR WORK

12. Each piece of the circle equals _____.

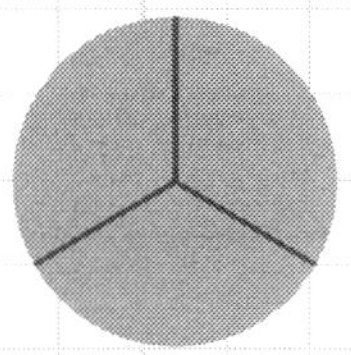

A. one-half

B. one-third

C. one-fourth

SHOW YOUR WORK

13. Which expression equals one whole?

A. Two Thirds

B. Three Thirds

C. Four Thirds

SHOW YOUR WORK

14. Which expression equals one whole?

A. Two Halves

B. Three Halves

C. Four Halves

SHOW YOUR WORK

15. Which expression equals one whole?

A. Two Fourths

B. Three Fourths

C. Four Fourths

SHOW YOUR WORK

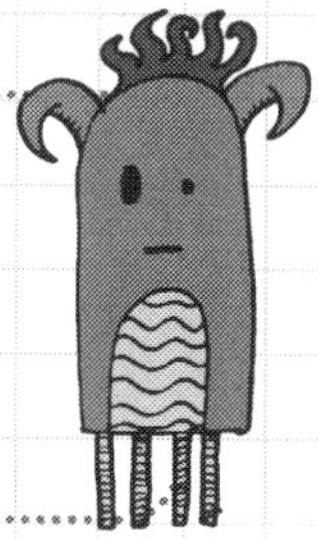

NOTES

4.2 | Chapter test

1. A triangle is a closed shape with ______ sides and ______ angles.

SHOW YOUR WORK

2. A pentagon is a closed shape with ______ straight sides.

SHOW YOUR WORK

3. A hexagon is a closed shape with ______ straight sides.

SHOW YOUR WORK

4. A quadrilateral is a closed shape with ______ straight sides.

SHOW YOUR WORK

4.2 | Chapter test

5. Circle all of the pentagons

A. 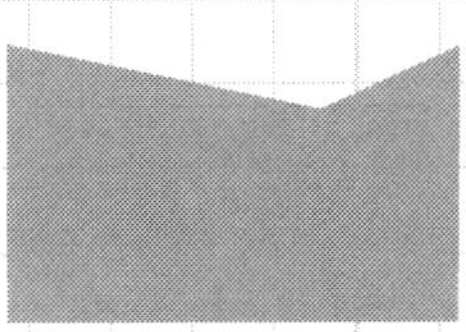

C. 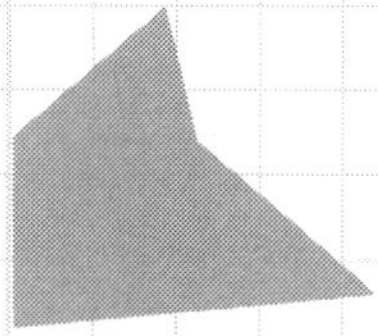

B. 

D. 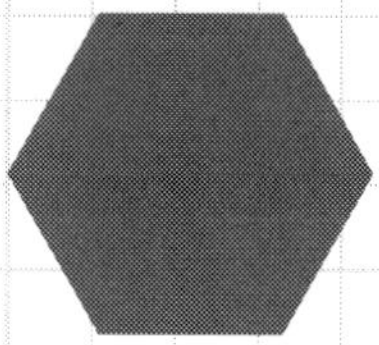

SHOW YOUR WORK

6. Circle all the hexagons

A. 

C. 

B. 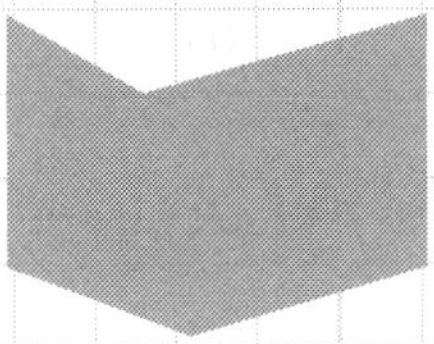

D. 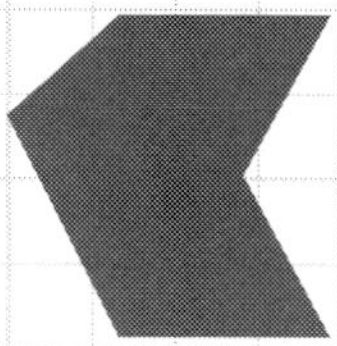

SHOW YOUR WORK

4.2 Chapter test

7. Draw three different quadrilaterals.

SHOW YOUR WORK

8. Draw a closed shape with 6 straight sides. What is the name of the shape?

SHOW YOUR WORK

9. Partition the rectangle into 3 rows and 5 columns.

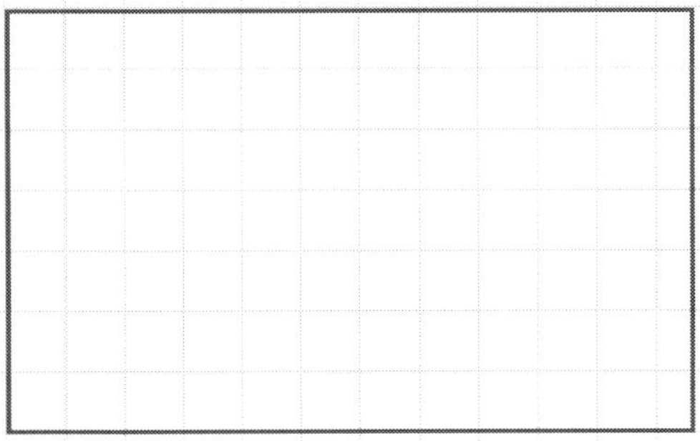

SHOW YOUR WORK

10. How many squares did you create in all?

SHOW YOUR WORK

4.2 | Chapter test

11. How many squares are in each row?

SHOW YOUR WORK

12. How many squares are in each column?

SHOW YOUR WORK

13. Partition the circle into halves.

SHOW YOUR WORK

14. Partition the circle into thirds.

SHOW YOUR WORK

ARGOPREP

4.2 | Chapter test

15. Partition the circle into fourths.

SHOW YOUR WORK

16. Partition the rectangle into 2 rows and 2 columns

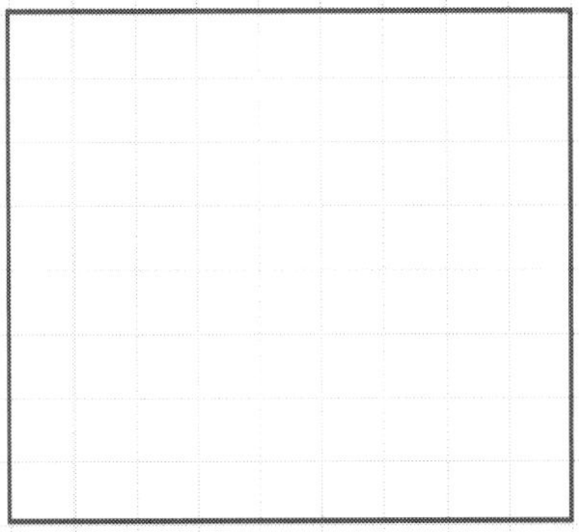

SHOW YOUR WORK

17. How many squares did you create in all?

SHOW YOUR WORK

18. How many squares are in each row?

SHOW YOUR WORK

19. How many squares are in each column?

SHOW YOUR WORK

20. Each square represents _____.

A. one-half

B. one-third

C. one-fourth

SHOW YOUR WORK

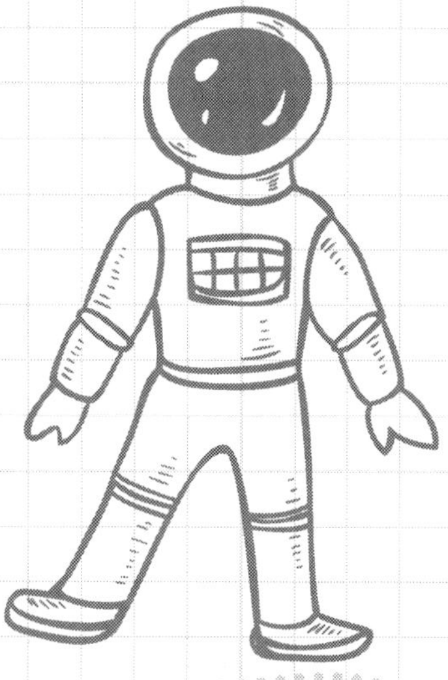

NOTES

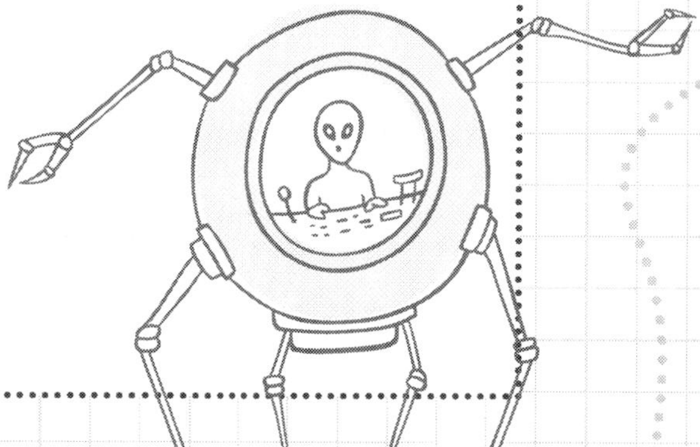

Chapter 5 :
Mixed Assessment

5 | Mixed Assessment

1. There are **45** oranges and **26** apples in the fruit basket. How many pieces of fruit are in the basket?

SHOW YOUR WORK

2. Baylee uses **35** chocolate chips for her cookie dough. She adds **25** more chocolate chips after mixing the dough together. How many chocolate chips did she use in all?

SHOW YOUR WORK

3. It snows **14** inches. **6** inches of the snow melts. Then it snows another **5** inches. How much snow is on the ground now?

SHOW YOUR WORK

4. Lara swims **32** laps of freestyle and **15** laps of backstroke at swim practice. How many laps does she swim all together?

SHOW YOUR WORK

5. Franny reads **52** pages of her book on Monday. She reads more pages on Tuesday. If she read a total of **95** pages, how many pages did she read on Tuesday?

SHOW YOUR WORK

6. 15 - 6 = ____ Explain your mental strategy.

SHOW YOUR WORK

7. 13 - 4 = ____ Explain your mental strategy.

SHOW YOUR WORK

8. 12 - 6 = ____ Explain your mental strategy.

SHOW YOUR WORK

9. 11 - 7 = ____ Explain your mental strategy

SHOW YOUR WORK

10. 18 + 4 = ____ Explain your mental strategy.

SHOW YOUR WORK

11. 17 + 7 = ____ Explain your mental strategy.

SHOW YOUR WORK

12. 14 + 93 = ____ Explain your mental strategy.

SHOW YOUR WORK

13. 15 + 6 = ____ Explain your mental strategy.

SHOW YOUR WORK

14. Is 19 an even number? Justify your thinking.

SHOW YOUR WORK

15. Is 16 an even number? Justify your thinking.

SHOW YOUR WORK

16. Is there an even number of strawberries? Justify your thinking.

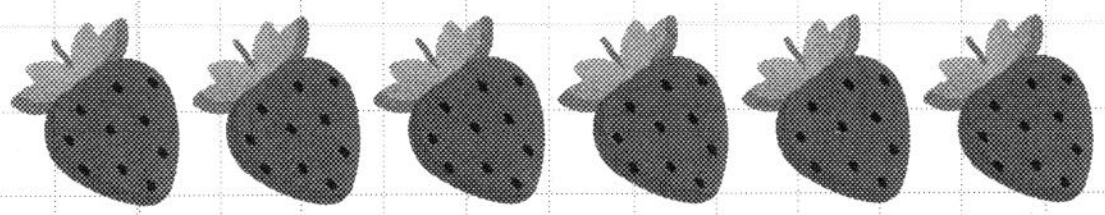

SHOW YOUR WORK

17. Is there an even number of hot dogs? Justify your thinking.

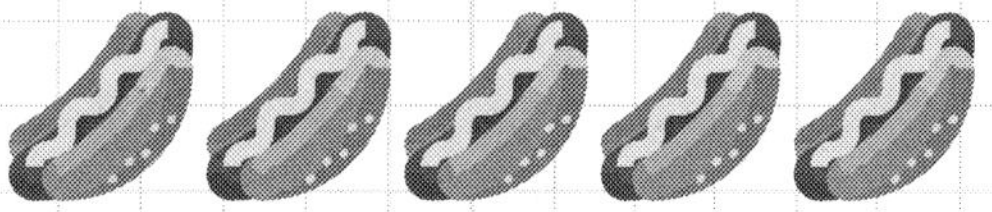

SHOW YOUR WORK

18. Write an equation to represent the total number of hearts.

SHOW YOUR WORK

19. Write an equation to represent the total number of stars.

SHOW YOUR WORK

20. Write an equation to represent the total number of diamonds.

SHOW YOUR WORK

5 | Mixed Assessment

21. Draw a rectangle with 2 rows of circles and 3 columns of circles.

SHOW YOUR WORK

22. How many circles are in your rectangle?

SHOW YOUR WORK

23. Draw a rectangle with 4 rows of circles and 4 columns of circles.

SHOW YOUR WORK

24. How many circles are in your rectangle?

SHOW YOUR WORK

25. Count by 100s starting at 150. Fill in the blanks

150, ____, ____, ____

SHOW YOUR WORK

26. Count by 10s starting at 150. Fill in the blanks

150, ____, ____, ____

SHOW YOUR WORK

27. Count by 5s starting at 150. Fill in the blanks

150, ____, ____, ____

SHOW YOUR WORK

28. Represent the number 487 using tens and ones.

_____ tens _____ ones

SHOW YOUR WORK

29. What number represents the same amount as 2 hundreds + 9 tens + 1 ones?

SHOW YOUR WORK

30. Fill in the blanks to make the equation true.

____ = 4 hundreds + 13 tens + 6 ones

SHOW YOUR WORK

31. Which expressions represent the same amount as 534?

A. 5 + 3 + 4

B. 50 + 3 + 4

C. 500 + 30 + 4

SHOW YOUR WORK

32. 612 ____ 621

A. >

B. <

C. =

SHOW YOUR WORK

33. 206 ____ 20 tens + 6 ones

A. >

B. <

C. =

SHOW YOUR WORK

34. 37 ____ 30 tens + 7 ones

A. >

B. <

C. =

SHOW YOUR WORK

35. Order the numbers from least to greatest: 7, 407, 47, 470

_____, _____, _____, _____

SHOW YOUR WORK

36. Order the numbers from least to greatest: 217, 712, 721, 271

_____, _____, _____, _____

SHOW YOUR WORK

37. What is 100 less than 512?

SHOW YOUR WORK

38. What is 300 more than 512?

SHOW YOUR WORK

39. What is 20 more than 349?

SHOW YOUR WORK

40. What is 60 less than 683?

SHOW YOUR WORK

5 | Mixed Assessment

41. 52 + 37 = _____ Show your work

SHOW YOUR WORK

42. 52 + 10 + 43 + 30 = _____

SHOW YOUR WORK

43. 45 + 55 + 65 + 16 = _____

SHOW YOUR WORK

44. 775 - 163 = _____ Show your work.

SHOW YOUR WORK

45. 334 - 132 = _____ Show your work.

SHOW YOUR WORK

46. The lizards lay **76** eggs in the morning. They lay **27** more in the afternoon and **64** more before nightfall. How many eggs did the chickens lay in all? Explain your strategy for solving the problem.

SHOW YOUR WORK

47. There are **63** kids at the pool. **17** kids leave. How many kids remain at the pool? Explain your strategy for solving the problem.

SHOW YOUR WORK

Use a ruler for questions **48- 52**

48. What is the length of the caterpillar?

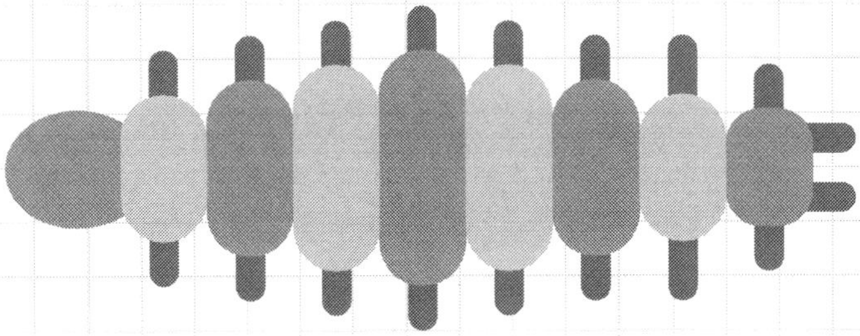

________ cm

SHOW YOUR WORK

49. What is the height of the caterpillar?

________ cm

SHOW YOUR WORK

50. What is the length of the caterpillar?

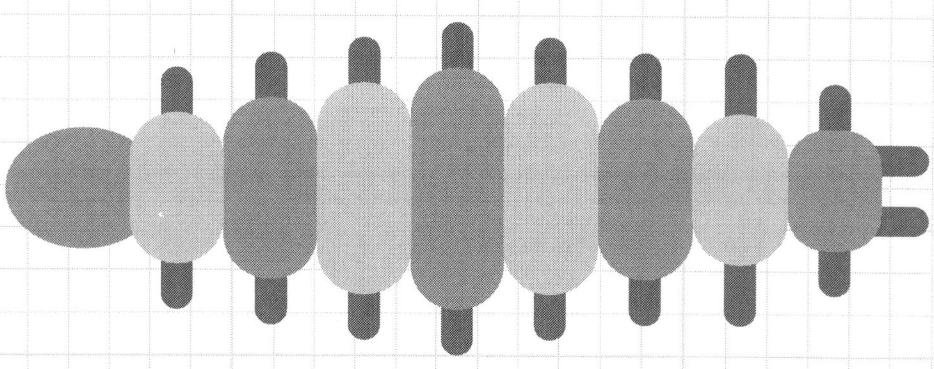

______ in

SHOW YOUR WORK

51. What is the height of the caterpillar?

________ in

SHOW YOUR WORK

52. How much longer is Line A than Line B?

SHOW YOUR WORK

Use the conversion chart to answer questions 53 - 56

Conversion Chart
1 feet = 12 inches
1 yard = 3 feet
1 meter = 100 cm

53. The field is 7 yards. How many feet is the field?

SHOW YOUR WORK

54. The garden is 6 feet long. What is the length in inches?

SHOW YOUR WORK

55. The flower is 24 inches tall. What is its height in feet?

SHOW YOUR WORK

56. The athlete swims 500 cm. How many meters does she swim?

SHOW YOUR WORK

57. Kara has two ribbons. One ribbon is **52** cm long. The other ribbon is **46** cm long. What is the length of both ribbons combined? Write an equation to solve the problem.

SHOW YOUR WORK

58. There are **33** students in Ms. Tompkin's class. **7** move away before winter break. **4** more move away during spring break. How many students are left in Ms. Tompkin's class after spring break? Use a number line to solve the problem.

SHOW YOUR WORK

59. There are **11** people at the party. **2** adults arrive at the party late. They bring **2** toddlers and **1** baby with them. How many people are at the party in all? Use a number line to solve the problem.

SHOW YOUR WORK

60. Lara has **5** one-dollar bills, **2** five-dollar bill and **3** ten-dollar bills. How much money does she have in all?

SHOW YOUR WORK

5 | Mixed Assessment

61. Show two ways to make 35¢ using pennies, nickels, dimes and quarters.

SHOW YOUR WORK

62. Show two ways to make 81¢ using pennies, nickels, dimes and quarters.

SHOW YOUR WORK

63. What is the total value of the coins below?

SHOW YOUR WORK

64. What is the total value of the coins below?

SHOW YOUR WORK

5 | Mixed Assessment

65. Draw the hands on the clock to show 7:25

SHOW YOUR WORK

66. Draw the hands on the clock to show 11:10

SHOW YOUR WORK

67. What time is shown on the clock below?

SHOW YOUR WORK

5 | Mixed Assessment

68. What time is shown on the clock below?

SHOW YOUR WORK

69. Gretchen measured her flowers. The lengths were 14, 14, 14, 18 and 21 inches. Create a line plot of the lengths.

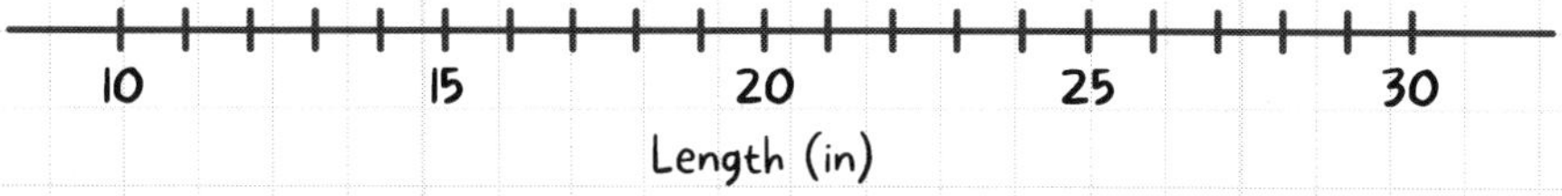

SHOW YOUR WORK

70. Laura measured five sticks. The lengths were 15, 18, 21, 21, 27 and 27 centimeters. Create a line plot of the lengths.

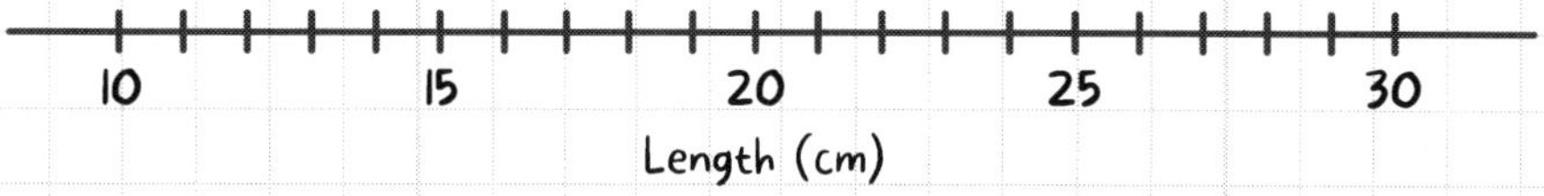

SHOW YOUR WORK

Use the chart below to answer questions 71 - 73

Favorite Season	Student Votes
Winter	12
Spring	5
Summer	13
Fall	6

71. Create a bar graph for the data.

SHOW YOUR WORK

72. Which season received the most votes?

SHOW YOUR WORK

73. Which season received the fewest votes?

SHOW YOUR WORK

Use the chart below to answer questions 74 - 78

Student	Number of Cupcakes Eaten
Craig	7
Evie	4
Kyle	2
Lashonda	5

74. Create a picture graph for the data.

SHOW YOUR WORK

75. Which student ate the most cupcakes?

SHOW YOUR WORK

76. Which student ate the fewest cupcakes?

SHOW YOUR WORK

77. How many more cupcakes did Craig eat than Kyle?

SHOW YOUR WORK

78. How many cupcakes did the students eat all together?

SHOW YOUR WORK

79. Draw a closed shape with 5 straight sides. What is the name of the shape?

SHOW YOUR WORK

80. Draw a closed shape with 3 straight sides and 3 angles. What is the name of the shape?

SHOW YOUR WORK

81. Partition the rectangle into **5** rows and **3** columns

SHOW YOUR WORK

82. How many squares did you create in all?

SHOW YOUR WORK

83. How many squares are in each row?

SHOW YOUR WORK

84. How many squares are in each column?

SHOW YOUR WORK

85. Partition the rectangle into 4 rows and 2 columns

SHOW YOUR WORK

86. How many squares did you create in all?

SHOW YOUR WORK

87. How many squares are in each row?

SHOW YOUR WORK

88. How many squares are in each column?

SHOW YOUR WORK

89. Partition the circle into thirds.

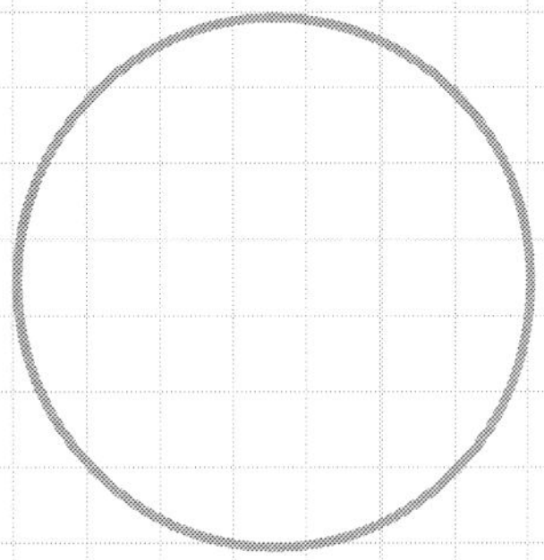

SHOW YOUR WORK

90. How many parts did you divide the circle into?

A. 2

B. 3

C. 4

D. 5

SHOW YOUR WORK

91. Shade one-third of the circle

SHOW YOUR WORK

92. Partition the circle into fourths.

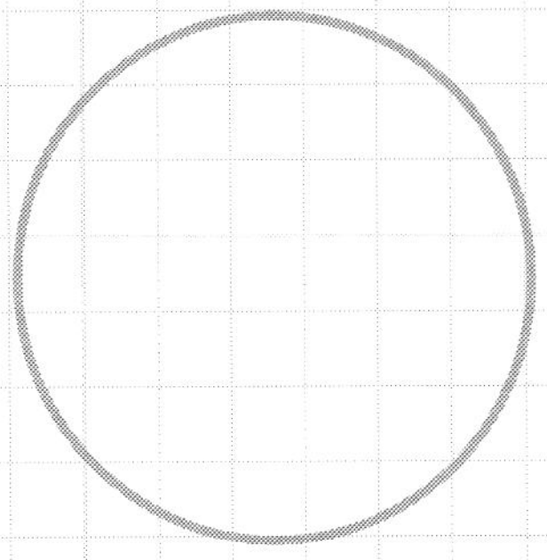

SHOW YOUR WORK

93. How many parts did you divide the circle into?

A. 2

B. 3

C. 4

D. 5

SHOW YOUR WORK

94. Shade one-fourth of the circle

SHOW YOUR WORK

95. Partition the circle into halves.

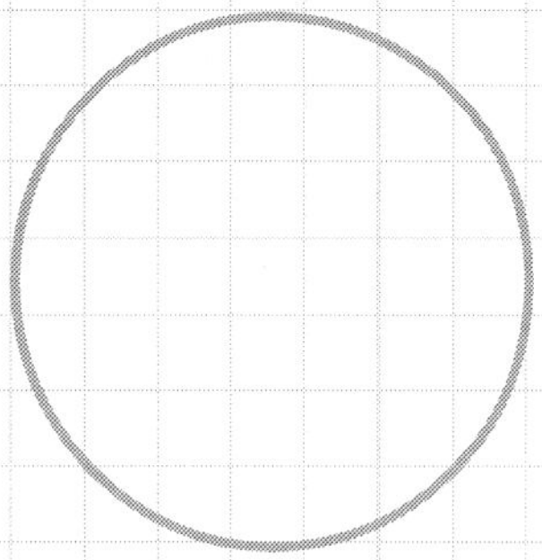

SHOW YOUR WORK

96. How many parts did you divide the circle into?

A. 2

B. 3

C. 4

D. 5

SHOW YOUR WORK

97. Shade one-half of the circle

SHOW YOUR WORK

5 | Mixed Assessment

98. Circle all of the triangles

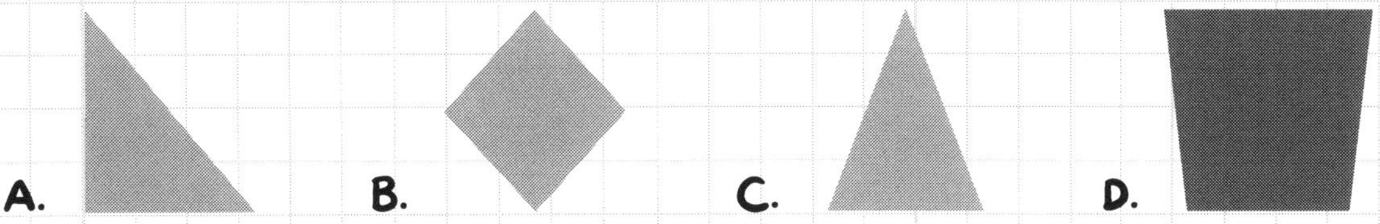

SHOW YOUR WORK

99. Circle all of the pentagons

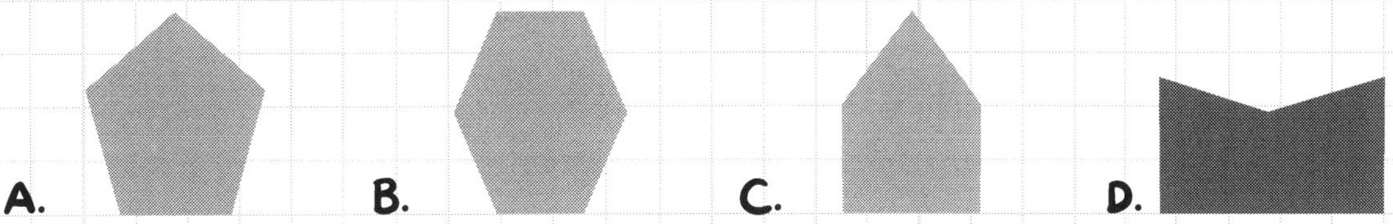

SHOW YOUR WORK

100. Circle all of the hexagons

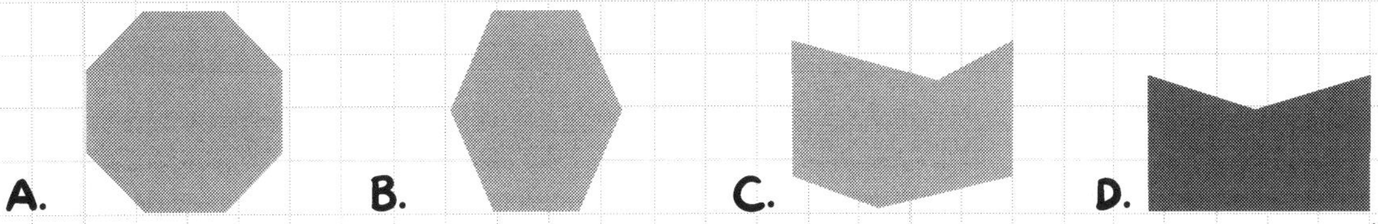

SHOW YOUR WORK

ANSWER SHEET

ANSWER SHEET

Chapter 1: Operations & Algebraic Thinking

1.1 Represent and Solve Word Problems

1. 30 ducks. This is an addition problem. The equation is 17 + 13 = 30.
2. 20 cookies. The change is unknown. Solve 25 - ____ = 5 by subtracting 5 from 25.
3. 14. The start is unknown. Solve the equation ____ + 46 = 60 by subtracting 46 from 60.
4. 63. This is an addition problem. The equation is 36 + 27 = ____.
5. 8. The addend is unknown. Solve 4 + ____ = 12 by subtracting 4 from 12.
6. 2 pieces. Subtract John's 13 from Jane's 15 to find out how many more pieces Jane has than John.
7. 4. Subtract Sloane's 17 from Nolan's 21 to find out how many fewer pencils Sloan has than Nolan.
8. 21. Subtract 30 from 51 to find out how many apples are left in the tree. The equation is 51 - 30 = ____.
9. 80. Add 63 to 17 to find our how many berries are in the pie. The equation is 63 + 17 = ____.
10. 32. Subtract 3 from 35 to find out how many pumpkins the kids took. The equation is 35 - ____ = 3.
11. 99. Add 56 to 43 to find the total number of apples. The equation is 56 + 43 = ____.
12. 12. Subtract 9 from 21 to find the weight of the black kitten. The equation is 9 + ____ = 21.
13. 24. The equation is 98 - 74 = ____.
14. 21. The equation is 86 - 65 = ____.
15. 55. The equation is 23 + 32 = ____.
16. 22. The equation is 24 - 8 + 6 = ____.
17. 85. The equation is 82 - 5 + 8 = ____.
18. 33. The equation is 39 - 9 + 3 = ____.
19. 88. The equation is 85 -2 + 5 = ____.
20. 3. This is a two-step problem. The equation is 12 - 3 - ____ = 6. First subtract 3 from 12. The answer is 9. Then subtract 6 from 9.

ANSWER SHEET

21. 45. This is a two-step problem. The equation is 54 - 5 - 4 = ____ .
22. 79. The equation is 93 - 14 = ____ .
23. 57. The equation is 34 + 23 = ____ .
24. 45. The equation is 32 + 13 = ____ .
25. 18. This is a two-step problem. The equation is 23 - 2 - 3 = ____ .
26. 27. Subtract 63 from 90. The equation is 63 + ____ = 90.
27. 40. The equation is 23 + 17 = ____ .
28. 20. This is a two-step problem. The equation is 35 - 9 - 6 = ____ .
29. 48. The equation is 96 - 48 = ____ .
30. 52. The equation is 67 - 15 = ____ .

1.2 Add and Subtract within 20

1. 20. Count on from 17.
2. 22. Decompose to make 9 a ten.
3. 37. Decompose to make 29 a thirty.
4. 17. Count on from 13.
5. 14. Decompose to make 8 a ten.
6. 14. Decompose to make 9 a ten.
7. 20. Count on from 18.
8. 18. Count on from 15.
9. 16. Decompose to make 11 a ten.
10. 20. Decompose to make 13 a ten.
11. 13. Create an easier problem by making 7 a ten.
12. 7. Use number relationships. 9 plus 7 is 16.
13. 9. Use number relationships. 5 plus 9 is 14.
14. 5. Create an easier problem by making 17 a twenty. 20 minus 15.
15. 11. Use a number relationship. 11 plus 8 is 19.
16. 2. Use a number relationship. 9 plus 2 is 11.
17. 7. Create an easier problem by making 5 a ten.
18. 2. Use number relationships . 6 plus 2 is 8.
19. 12. Use number relationships. 6 plus 12 is 18.
20. 7. Create an easier problem by making 19 a twenty.
21. 5. Use number relationships.

ANSWER SHEET

22. 14. Create an easier problem.
23. 14. Create an easier problem.
24. 8. Create an easier problem.
25. 13. Use number relationships.
26. 5. Count on.
27. 8. Decompose to make a ten.
28. 4. Count on.
29. 5. Decompose to make a ten.
30. 6. Decompose to make a ten.

1.3.A. Understanding Even and Odd Numbers

1. Odd. The objects can't be placed into two equal groups.
2. Even. The objects can be placed into two equal groups.
3. Odd. The objects can't be placed into two equal groups.
4. Even. 2 + 2 + 2 + 2 + 2 = 10
5. Odd. 2 + 2 + 1.
6. Odd. 2 + 2 + 2 + 1.
7. Even. 2 + 2 + 2 + 2.
8. Odd. 2 + 2 + 2 + 2 + 2 + 1.
9. Yes. 8 + 8 The number can be split into two equal groups.
10. No. The number can't be split into two equal groups.
11. No. The number can't be split into two equal groups.
12. Yes. The number can be split into two equal groups.
13. Yes. The number can be split into two equal groups.
14. No. The number can't be split into two equal groups.
15. No. The number can't be split into two equal groups.

1.3.B. Adding Equal Groups

1. 3 + 3 = 6. 2 rows of 3.
2. 2 + 2 + 2 = 6. 3 rows of 2.
3. 4 + 4 + 4 = 12. 3 rows of 4.
4. 5 + 5 + 5 + 5 = 20. 4 rows of 5.

ANSWER SHEET

5. 4 + 4 = 8. 2 rows of 4.
6. 2 + 2 + 2 + 2 = 8. 4 rows of 2.
7. 3 + 3 + 3 = 9. 3 rows of 3.
8. 5 + 5 = 10. 2 rows of 5.
9. 2 + 2 + 2 + 2 = 8. 4 rows of 2.
10. 5 + 5 + 5 = 15. 3 rows of 5.
11. 10. 2 + 2 + 2 + 2 + 2.
12. 12. 3 + 3 + 3 + 3.
13. 6. 2 + 2 + 2.
14. 4. 2 + 2.
15. 8. 2 + 2 + 2 + 2.

1.4 Chapter Test

1. 60. This is an addition problem. The equation is 37 + 23.
2. 70. This is an addition problem. The equation is 55 + 15.
3. 15. This is a two step problem. First subtract 5 from 12. Then add 8.
4. 60. This is an addition problem. The equation is 25 + 35.
5. 20. 65 + ____ = 85 Subtract 65 from 85 to find the missing addend.
6. 8. Use number relationships or make an easier problem.
7. 5. Use number relationships or make an easier problem.
8. 9. Use number relationships or make an easier problem.
9. 17. Count on or decompose.
10. 19. Count on or decompose.
11. 21. Count on or decompose.
12. No. It can't be split into two equal groups.
13. Yes. It can be split into two equal groups.
14. Yes. They can be split into two equal groups.
15. No. They cant be split into two equal groups.
16. 4 + 4. 2 rows of 4.
17. 3 + 3 + 3 + 3. 4 rows of 3.
18. 2 + 2 + 2. 3 rows of 2.
19. Answers may vary. Should have 5 rows of 2 circles.
20. Answers may vary. Should have 2 rows of 3 circles.

ANSWER SHEET

Chapter 2: Numbers & Operation in Base Ten

2.1.A. Understanding Three Digit Numbers

1. 10 tens 7 ones. A hundred is a group of 10 tens. There is 1 hundred in 107.
2. 21 tens 6 ones. A hundred is a group of 10 tens. There are 2 hundreds in 216. There is also one ten in 16.
3. 31 tens 4 ones. A hundred is a group of 10 tens. There are 3 hundreds in 314. There is also one ten in 14.
4. 14 tens 5 ones. A hundred is a group of 10 tens. There is 1 hundred in 145. There are also 4 tens in 45.
5. 32 tens 4 ones. A hundred is a group of 10 tens. There are 3 hundreds in 324. There are also 2 tens in 24.
6. 12 tens 3 ones. A hundred is a group of 10 tens. There is 1 hundred in 123. There are also 2 tens in 23.
7. 16 tens 5 ones. A hundred is a group of 10 tens. There is 1 hundred in 165. There are also 6 tens in 65.
8. 18 tens 9 ones. A hundred is a group of 10 tens. There is 1 hundred in 189. There are also 8 tens in 89.
9. 23 tens 5 ones. A hundred is a group of 10 tens. There are 2 hundreds in 235. There are also 3 tens in 35.
10. 37 tens 4 ones. A hundred is a group of 10 tens. There are 3 hundreds in 374. There are also 7 tens in 74.
11. 10. A hundred is a group of 10 tens. There is 1 hundred in 106.
12. 32. A hundred is a group of 10 tens. There are 3 hundreds in 326.
13. 30. A hundred is a group of 10 tens. There are 3 hundreds in 326.
14. 323. 20 tens for 200 plus 12 tens for 12 is 32 tens.
15. 3,565. 3400 + 160 + 5 = 3,565.

ANSWER SHEET

2.1.B. Skip Counting

1. 190, 195, 200, 205, 210, 215. The ones digit alternates between 0 and 5. We add 5 at a time.
2. 360, 370, 380, 390, 400, 410. The tens digit increases by 1 each time. We add 10 at a time.
3. 275, 375, 475, 575, 675, 775. The hundreds digit increases by 1 each time. We add 100 at a time.
4. 185, 190, 195, 200, 205. The ones digit alternates between 0 and 5. We add 5 at a time.
5. 195, 205, 215, 225. The tens digit increases by 1 each time. We add 10 at a time.
6. 185, 285, 385, 485, 585. The hundreds digit increases by 1 each time. We add 100 at a time.
7. C. The ones digit alternates between 0 and 5. We add 5 at a time.
8. B. The tens digit increases by 1 each time. We add 10 at a time.
9. C. The hundreds digit increases by 1 each time. We add 100 at a time.
10. 490, 390, 290, 190. The hundreds digit decreases by 1 each time. We subtract 100 at a time.
11. 555, 545, 535, 525, 515. The tens digit decreases by 1 each time. We subtract 10 at a time.
12. 375, 370, 365, 360, 355. The ones digit alternates between 0 and 5. We subtract 5 at a time.
13. 660, 560, 460, 360. The hundreds digit decreases by 1 each time. We subtract 100 at a time.
14. 680, 670, 660, 650, 640. The tens digit decreases by 1 each time. We subtract 10 at a time.
15. 860, 855, 850, 845, 840. The ones digit alternates between 0 and 5. We subtract 5 at a time.

ANSWER SHEET

2.1.C. Creating Three-Digit Numbers

1. A.
2. C.
3. A.
4. B.
5. A.
6. 127 = 1 hundreds + 2 tens + 7 ones.
7. 989 = 9 hundreds + 8 tens + 9 ones.
8. 117 = 1 hundreds + 1 tens + 7 ones.
9. 611 = 6 hundreds + 1 tens + 1 ones.
10. 647 = 6 hundreds + 4 tens + 7 ones.
11. 235 = 2 hundreds + 3 tens + 5 ones.
12. 618 = 6 hundreds + 1 tens + 8 ones.
13. 555 = 5 hundreds + 5 tens + 5 ones
14. 415 = 400 + 10 + 5.
15. 802 = 800 + 2.

2.1.D. Comparing Three Digit Numbers

1. B. The tens place is less.
2. C. 200 is equal to 20 tens, which is the same as 200
3. B. The tens place is less.
4. A. The tens place is greater 412 > 409.
5. C. The numbers are equal.
6. B. The tens place is less.
7. A. 100 + 20 +1 is equal to 121. 12 tens is equal to 120.
8. C. Both are equal to 100.
9. A. 383 is greater than 283.
10. 26, 206, 244, 266. Use place value to determine the order.
11. 62. 66. 116. 611. Use place value to determine the order.
12. 25, 66, 205, 485. Use place value to determine the order.

ANSWER SHEET

13. 25, 52, 502, 520. Use place value to determine the order.
14. 24. 42, 406, 642. Use place value to determine the order.
15. 23, 32, 723, 732. Use place value to determine the order.

2.2.A. Adding and Subtracting within 100

1. 91. 50 + 30 = 80 and 6 + 5 = 11. 80 + 11 = 91. So, 56 + 35 = 91.
2. 61. 40 + 10 = 50 and 9 + 2 = 11. 50 + 11 = 61. So, 49 + 12 = 61.
3. 88. 60 + 20 = 80. 2 + 6 = 8. 80 + 8 = 88 So, 62 + 26 = 88.
4. 68. 20 + 40 = 60 and 3 + 5 = 8. 60 + 8 = 68. So, 23 + 45 = 68.
5. 96. 30 + 60 = 90 and 3 + 3 = 6. 90 + 6 = 96. So, 33 + 63 = 96.
6. 42. 50 - 10 = 40 and 4 - 2 = 2. 40 and 2 = 42. So, 54 - 12 = 42.
7. 50. 60 - 10 = 50. 2- 2 = 0. So, 62 - 12 = 50.
8. 32. 40 - 10 = 30. 5 - 3 = 2. 30 and 3 = 33. So, 45 - 13 = 32.
9. 38. 50 - 10 = 40 and 40 - 2 = 38. So, 50 - 12 = 38.
10. 34. 80 - 50 = 30 and 8 - 4 = 4. 30 and 4 = 34. So, 88 - 54 =34.
11. 71. Add 25 to 46.
12. 97. Add 45 to 52.
13. 43. Subtract 35 from 78 cookies.
14. 12. Subtract 24 from 36.
15. 45. Subtract 45 from 90

2.2.B. Adding Strings of Numbers

1. 158. First add 43 and 62. Then add 21 and 32. Combine the sums
2. 91. Use place value to add the numbers.
3. 135. Break apart and add to make an easier problem.
4. 114. Use place value to add the numbers.
5. 150. Use place value to add the numbers.
6. 134. Use place value to add the numbers.
7. 116. Use place value to add the numbers.
8. 113. Use place value to add the numbers.

9. 147. First add 67 to 39. Then add 26 to 15. Combine the sums to get 147.
10. 101. First add 42 and 27. Then add 32.
11. 173. Use place value to add the numbers.
12. 90. Use place value to add the numbers.
13. 169. The equation is 56 + 35 + 78. Add 56 and 78 first. Then add 35.
14. 131. The equation is 35 + 23 + 47 +26. Add 23 and 47 first. Then add 35 and 26. Combine the sums to get 131.
15. 162. The equation is 42 + 74 + 46. Add 74 and 46 first. Then add 42 to the sum.

2.2.C. Add and Subtract within 1,000

1. A. 314 + 416 = 730.
2. B. Each digit is represented by its place value.
3. C. Each digit is represented by its place value.
4. 309. Use a model to visualize the 100s, 10s and 1s.
5. 71. Use a model to visualize the 100s, 10s and 1s.
6. 162. Use a model to visualize the 100s, 10s and 1s.
7. 742. Use a model to visualize the 100s, 10s and 1s.
8. 440. Use a model to visualize the 100s, 10s and 1s.
9. 444. Use a model to visualize the 100s, 10s and 1s.
10. 957. Use a model to visualize the 100s, 10s and 1s.
11. 528. Use a model to visualize the 100s, 10s and 1s.
12. 800. Use a model to visualize the 100s, 10s and 1s.
13. 464. Use a model to visualize 587 - 123.
14. 759. Use a model to visualize 327 + 432.
15. 171. 837 - 234 - 432 = 171

2.2.D. Mentally Adding and Subtracting 10s and 100s

1. 833. The tens digit decreases by one.
2. 702. The tens digit increases by three.
3. 143. The hundreds digit decreases by four.
4. 813. The hundreds digit increases by one.

5. 405. The hundreds digit decreases by two.
6. 910. The hundreds digit increases by one.
7. 919. The tens digit decreases by one.
8. 537. The hundreds digit increases by three.
9. 460. The hundreds digit increases by two.
10. 902. The tens digit decreases by one.
11. 812. The hundreds digit decreases by one.
12. 361. The tens digit increases by 5.
13. 343. The hundreds digit increases by one.
14. 102. The tens digit decreases by two.
15. 322. The hundreds digit decreases by one.

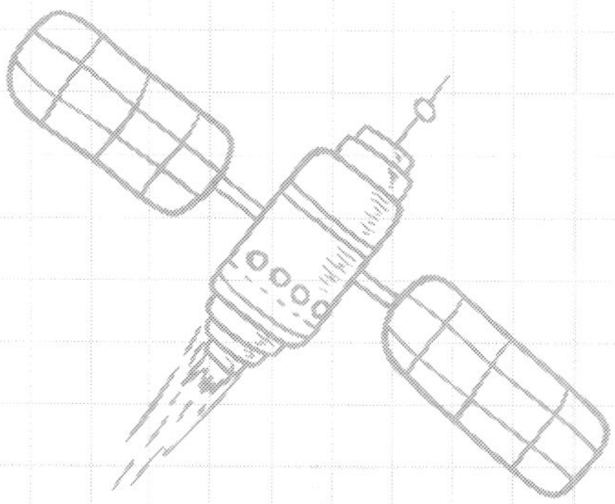

2.2.E. Explaining Different Strategies

1. 29. Explanations may vary but should demonstrate a knowledge of place value or operations.
2. 45. Explanations may vary but should demonstrate a knowledge of place value or operations.
3. 41. Explanations may vary but should demonstrate a knowledge of place value or operations.
4. 9. Explanations may vary but should demonstrate a knowledge of place value or operations.
5. 22. Explanations may vary but should demonstrate a knowledge of place value or operations.
6. 108. Explanations may vary but should demonstrate a knowledge of place value or operations.
7. 98. Explanations may vary but should demonstrate a knowledge of place value or operations.
8. 77. Explanations may vary but should demonstrate a knowledge of place value or operations.
9. 129. Explanations may vary but should demonstrate a knowledge of place value or operations.
10. 80. Explanations may vary but should demonstrate a knowledge of place value or operations.

11. 78. The equation is 24 + 54. Explanations may vary but should demonstrate a knowledge of place value or operations.
12. 108. The equation is 36 + 45 + 27. Explanations may vary but should demonstrate a knowledge of place value or operations.
13. 127. The equation is 23 + 45 + 59. Explanations may vary but should demonstrate a knowledge of place value or operations.
14. 45. The equation is 82 - 37. Explanations may vary but should demonstrate a knowledge of place value or operations.
15. 41. The equation is 95 - 54. Explanations may vary but should demonstrate a knowledge of place value or operations.

2.3. Chapter Test

1. 21 tens 7 ones. There are 20 tens in 200, plus 1 ten in 17, plus 7 ones.
2. 412. There are 3 hundreds, plus another hundred from the 11 tens, which makes 4 hundred. That leaves 1 ten and 2 ones.
3. 655, 755, 855, 955. The hundreds digit increases by one. Add 100 each time.
4. 655, 665, 675, 685. The tens digit increases by one. Add 10 each time.
5. 655, 660, 665, 670. The ones digit alternates between 0 and 5. Add 5 each time.
6. 622. There are 5 hundreds, plus 1 hundred from the 12 tens for 6 hundreds. Then add 2 tens and 2 ones.
7. C. The number is expressed in expanded form, which represents place value.
8. A. The tens digit is greater.
9. C. The numbers are equal.
10. 17, 71, 107, 702. Use place value to order the numbers.
11. 212. The hundreds digit decreases by one.
12. 110.
13. 62. 94 -32 = 62
14. 412. The hundreds digit decreases by two.
15. 553. The tens digit decreases by three.
16. 138. First add 14 and 36. Then add 33 and 55. Combine the sums to get 138.

ANSWER SHEET

17. 180.
First add 64 and 16. Then add 75 and 25. Combine the sums to get 180.
18. 422. Explanations may vary but should demonstrate a knowledge of place value or operations.
19. 202. Explanations may vary but should demonstrate a knowledge of place value or operations.
20. 126. The equation is 23 + 47 + 56. Explanations may vary but should demonstrate a knowledge of place value or operations.

Chapter 3: Measurement & Data

3.1.A. Using Tools to Measure

1. A. The object is small enough for a ruler.
2. B. The object is larger than a ruler.
3. A. The object is small enough for a ruler.
4. A. The object is small enough for a ruler.
5. B. The object is larger than a ruler.
6. A. Line the edge of the paper clip up with the zero hashmark on the ruler.
7. 3 cm. Line the bottom of the laundry machine up with the zero hashmark on the centimeter side of the ruler.
8. 2 cm. Line the edge of the tape dispenser up with the zero hashmark on the centimeter side of the ruler.
9. 5 cm. Line the edge of the pencil up with the zero hashmark on the centimeter side of the ruler.
10. 1 in. Line the bottom of the chair up with t the zero hashmark on the inch side of the ruler.
11. 3 in. Line the bottom of the book up with the zero hashmark on the inch side of the ruler.
12. B. Line the edge of the line up with the zero hashmark on the centimeter side of the ruler.
13. A. Line the edge of the line up with the zero hashmark on the centimeter side of the ruler.

ANSWER SHEET

14. B. Line the edge of the line up with the zero hasmark on the centimeter side of the ruler.
15. A. Line the edge of the line up with the zero hasmark on the centimeter side of the ruler.

3.1.B. Understanding Different Measurements

1. A.
2. D.
3. Centimeters are smaller units of measurement. It takes more centimeters than inches to get from the bottom of the street lamp to the top.
4. A.
5. D.
6. Centimeters are smaller units of measurement. It takes more centimeters than inches to get from the bottom of the hydrant to the top.
7. D. There are 12 inches in each foot. Since the house is 2 feet, we can write the equation 12 + 12, which equals 24.
8. A. There are 3 feet in each yard. Since there are 5 yards, we can write the equation 3 + 3+ 3+ 3+ 3, which equals 15.
9. C. There are 100 centimeters in each meter. Since there are 2 meters, we can write the equation 100 + 100, which equals 200.
10. B. There are 12 inches in each foot. Since there are 5 feet, we can write the equation as 12 + 12 + 12 + 12 + 12, which equals 60.
11. B. There are 100 cm in each meter. Since there are 2 hundreds in 200, we know that there are 2 meters.
12. 21. There are 3 feet in each yard. Since there are 7 yards, we can write the equation as 3 + 3 + 3 + 3 + 3 + 3 + 3, which equals 21.
13. 9. There are 3 feet in each yard. Since there are 3 yards, we can write the equation as 3 + 3 + 3, which equals 9.
14. Answers may vary, but should explain that feet are smaller units than yards.
15. Answers may vary, but should explain that inches are smaller units than feet.

ANSWER SHEET

3.1.C. Estimating Lengths

1. B. Half of the pumpkin is 1 ft. So the whole pumpkin is 1 ft + 1 ft, which equals 2 ft.
2. B. Half of the flower is 2 in. So the whole flower is 2 in + 2 in, which equals 4 in.
3. A. Half of the pea is 1 cm. So the whole pea is 1 cm + 1 cm, which equals 2 cm.
4. C. The caterpillar is about three lines long. The equation is 2 cm + 2 cm + 2 cm, which equals 6 cm.
5. 6 in. The water bottle twice the height of the small water bottle. The equation is 3 in + 3 in, which equals 6 in.
6. 1 foot. The big sub is the length of about 4 small subs.
7. 5 in. The small pancake stack is half the size of the large pancake stack. We know that 5 + 5 equals 10. So, the answer is 5 inches.
8. 6 in. The big burger is the height of three small burgers. The equation is 2 in + 2 in + 2 in, which equals 6 in.
9. 2ft. The big flamingo is about the height of two small flamingos. The equation is 1 ft + 1 ft, which equals 2 ft.
10. 10 in. The big stack is about the height of two small stacks. We know that there are 2 tens in 20. So there is 1 ten in the smaller stack.
11. C. Centimeters and inches are usually too small. The best estimate is 25 meters .
12. C. Centimeters and inches are usually too small. The best estimate is 50 feet.
13. A. Inches and yards are usually too large. The best estimate is 25 centimeters.
14. B. Inches are usually too small. Meters are usually too big. The best estimate is 10 feet.
15. A. Inches and meters are usually too big for a nail. The best estimate is 10 centimeters.

ANSWER SHEET

3.1.D. Comparing Measurements

1. 2 inches. Use an inch ruler to measure the line.
2. 5 inches. Use an inch ruler to measure the line.
3. 3 inches. 5 inches - 2 inches = 3 inches.
4. Figure C. Figure C is 3 inches.
5. Figure B. Figure B is 1 inch.
6. 1 inch. Figure A is 2 inches and Figure B is 1 inch. 2 inch - 1 inch = 1 inch.
7. 2 inches. Figure C is 3 inches and Figure B is 1 inch. 3 inches - 1 inches = 2 inches.
8. 1 inch. Figure C is 3 inches. Figure A is 2 inches. 3 inches - 2 inches = 1 inch.
9. B. Figure B is 4 cm.
10. C. Figure C is 2 cm.
11. 2 cm. 4 cm - 2 cm = 2 cm.
12. 1 cm. Figure B is 4 cm and Figure A is 3 cm.
13. 1 cm. Figure C is 2 cm and Figure A is 3 cm.
14. 7 yards. 5 yards + 2 yards.
15. 10 feet. 13 feet - 3 feet.

3.2.A. Using Addition and Subtraction to Solve Word Problems

1. 58 cm. The equation is 36 + 22 = ____ .
2. 100 m. The equation is 50 + 25 + 25 = ____ .
3. 100 yards. The equation is 45 + 55 = ____ .
4. 90 yards. The equation is 76 + 14 = ____ .
5. 88 cm. The equation is 42 + 46 = ____ .
6. 26 cm. The equation is 60 - 34 = ____ .
7. 37 in. The equation is 63 - 26 = ____ .
8. 22 meters. The equation is 85 - 63 = ____ .
9. 18 cm. The equation is 72 - 54 = ____ .
10. 13 inches. The equation is 45 - 32 = ____ .
11. 15 inches. The equation is 49 - 34 = ____ .

ANSWER SHEET

12. 71 inches. The equation is 34 + 37 = ____ .
13. 17 inches. The equation is 54 - 37 = ____ .
14. 28 inches. The equation is 62 - 34 = ____ .
15. 96 inches. The equation is 62 + 34 = ____ .

3.2.B. Using Number Lines to Solve Word Problems

1. A. This is an addition problem so the numbers will increase. Start at 10. Move forward 2 hashmarks for the squirrels, 3 for the rabbits and 1 for the frog.
2. B. This is an addition problem so the numbers will increase. Start at 30. Move forward 3 hashmarks for the students in February. 2 for the students in March and 4 for the students in May.
3. A. This is an addition problem so the numbers will increase. Start at 80. Move forward 3 hashmarks for the kids who join at snack, 3 for the kids who join after snack and 2 for the kids who join at lunch.
4. A. This is an addition problem so the numbers will increase. Start at 10. Move forward 2 hashmark for Sarah's blocks, 3 hashmarks for Lara's blocks and 1 haskmark for Fran's block
5. A. This is an addition problem so the numbers will increase. Start at 0. Move forward 3 hashmarks for the carrot cupcakes, 3 for the chocolate cupcakes and 2 for the vanilla cupcakes.
6. 32.

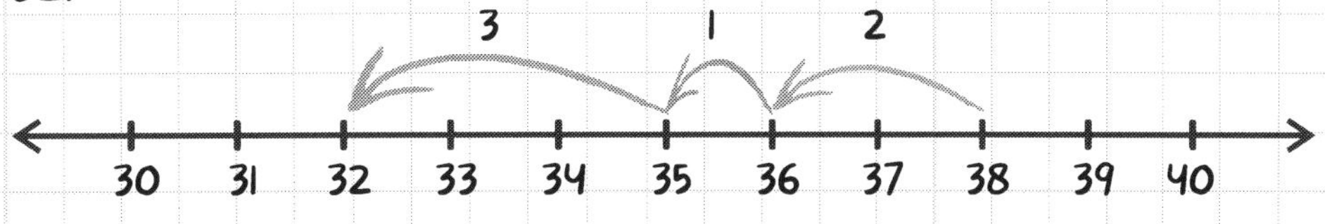

7. 76.

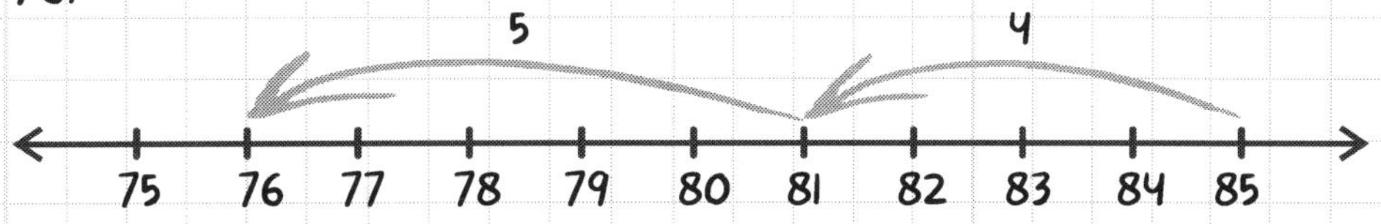

ANSWER SHEET

8. 12.

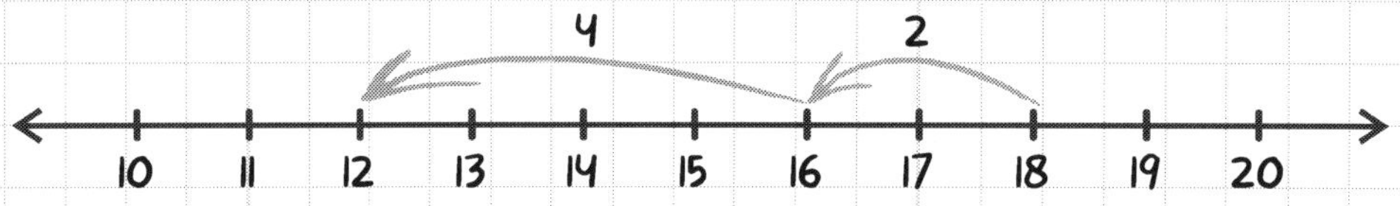

9. 81.

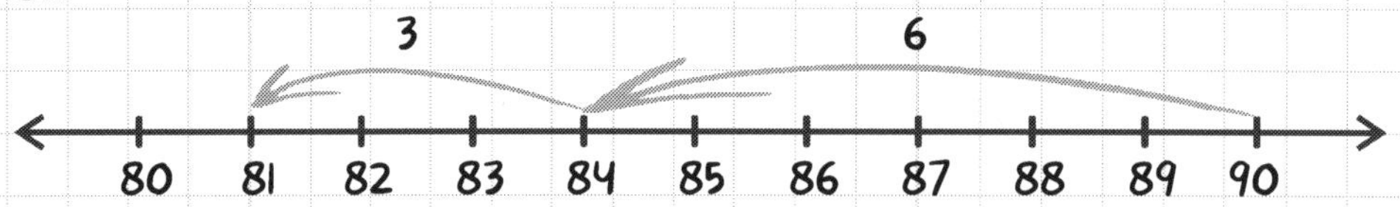

10. 31.

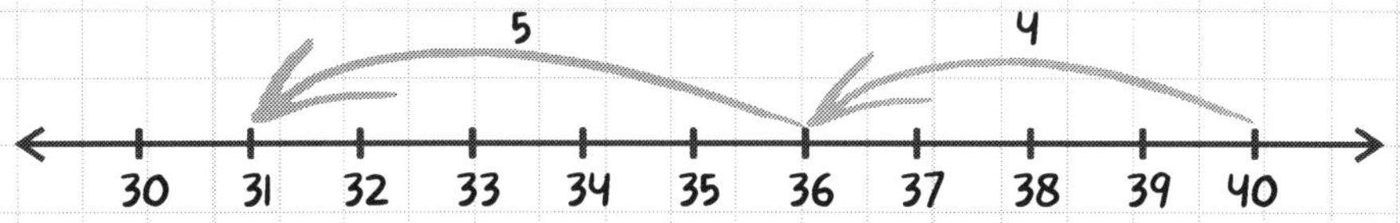

11. 17. This is a subtraction problem so the numbers will decrease. Start at 26. Since 9 people get off you can hop back 9 hashmarks. You could also hop back 10 since it's easier to work with, and then add 1.
12. 42. This is an addition problem so the numbers will increase. Start at 35. Hop forward 7 hashmarks. You could also break 7 into 5 and 2 to make hopping easier.
13. 52. This is a subtraction problem so the numbers will decrease. Start at 64. Hop back 12 hashmarks. You could also break 12 into 10 and 2 to make hopping easier.
14. 56. This is an addition problem so the numbers will increase. Start at 47. Hop forward 4 hasmarks for the books read over fall break. Hop forward 5 hashmarks for the books read over winter break. You could also hop forward 10 since 5 and 4 are close to ten, and then jump back one.
15. 55. This is a subtraction problem so the numbers will decrease. Start at 70. Hop back 11 for the first set of birds that fly away. Hop back 4 for the second set of birds that fly away. You could also break 11 into 10 and 1 to make hopping easier. If you do this, you'll hop 10 spaces then 5 spaces.

ANSWER SHEET

3.3.A. Working with Time

1. 9:10. The hour hand is at the 9. Since the short hand is at the 2, we skip count by 5 twice (5 .... 10).
2. 9:35. The hour hand is at the 9. Since the short hand is at the 7, we skip count by 5s seven times (5 .... 10 .... 15 .... 20 .... 25 .... 30 .... 35).
3. 6:15. The hour hand is at the 6. Since the short hand is at the 3, we skip count by 5s three times (5 .... 10 .... 15).
4. 6:55. The hour hand is at the 6. Since the short hand is at the 11, we skip count by 5s eleven times (5 .... 10 .... 15 .... 20 .... 25 .... 30 .... 35 .... 40 .... 45 .... 50 .... 55).
5. 8:40. The hour hand is at the 8. Since the short hand is at the 8, we skip count by 5s eight times (5 .... 10 .... 15 .... 20 .... 25 .... 30 .... 35 .... 40).
6. A. The hour hand is just past the 1, and the minute hand is at the 3 (5 .... 10 .... 15).
7. B. The hour hand is just past the 3, and the minute hand is at the 5 (5 .... 10 .... 15 .... 20 .... 25).
8. B. The hour hand is just past the 2, and the minute hand is at the 2 (5 .... 10).
9. A. The hour hand is just past the 1, and the minute hand is at the 3 (5 .... 10 .... 15).
10. A. The hour hand is just past the 7, and the minute hand is at the 9 (5 .... 10 .... 15 .... 20 .... 25 .... 30 .... 35 .... 40 .... 45).
11. A. The hour hand is just past the 4, and the minute hand is at the 4 (5 .... 10 .... 15 .... 20).
12. The hour hand should fall between the 1 and 2. The minute hand should be on the 6 (5 .... 10 .... 15 .... 20 .... 25 .... 30).

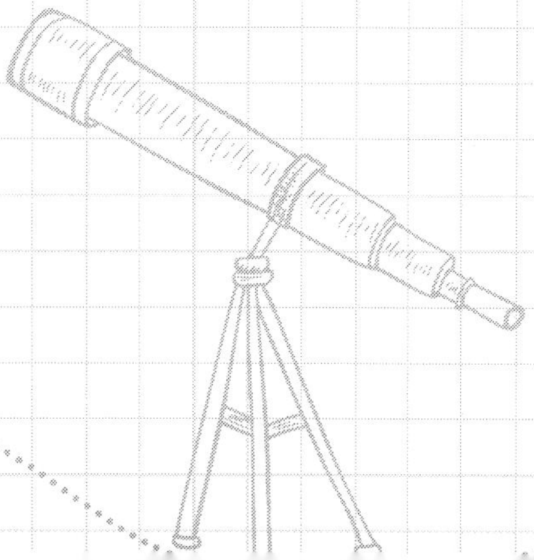

ANSWER SHEET

13. The hour hand should fall between the 5 and 6. The minute hand should be on the 9 (5 .... 10 .... 15 .... 20 .... 25 .... 30 .... 35 .... 40 .... 45).

14. The hour hand should fall between the 2 and 3. The minute hand should be on the 11 (5 .... 10 .... 15 .... 20 .... 25 .... 30 .... 35 .... 40 .... 45 .... 50 .... 55).

15. The hour hand should fall between the 4 and 5. The minute hand should be on the 9 (5 .... 10 .... 15 .... 20 .... 25 .... 30 .... 35 .... 40 .... 45).

3.3.B. Working with Money

1. Answers may vary.
   Possible answers include 1 quarter and 1 penny; 2 dimes ,1 nickel and 1 penny; or 5 nickels and 1 penny.
2. Answers may vary. Possible answers include 2 quarters and 1 penny; 5 dimes and 1 penny; or 10 nickels and 1 penny.
3. Answers may vary. Possible answers include 1 quarter, 1 dime and 2 pennies; 3 dimes ,1 nickel and 2 pennies; or 7 nickels and 2 pennies.

ANSWER SHEET

4. Answers may vary. Possible answers include 1 dime, 1 nickel and 2 pennies; 1 dime and 6 pennies; or 3 nickels and 1 penny.
5. Answers may vary. Possible answers include 3 quarters, 1 nickel and 3 pennies; 8 dimes and 3 pennies; or 3 quarters and 8 pennies.
6. $43. There are 3 ones 2 fives and 3 tens. We can write this as 3 + 10 + 30 = ____ .
7. $17. There are 2 ones and 3 fives. We can write this as 2 + 15 = ____ .
8. $62. There are 7 ones, 1 five, and 5 tens. We can write this as 7 + 5 + 50 = ____ .
9. $45. There are 5 fives and 2 tens. We can write this as 25 + 20 = ____ .
10. $60. There are 5 fives, 3 tens and 5 ones. We can write this as 25 + 30 + 5 = ____ .
11. 37¢. There are 3 dimes, 1 nickel, and 2 pennies. We can write this as 30 + 5 + 2 = ____ .
12. 36¢. There are 1 twenty-five, 1 ten and 1 one. We can write this as 25 + 10 + 1 = ____ .
13. 12¢. There are 2 fives and 2 ones. We can write this as 10 + 2 = ____ .
14. 87¢. There are 3 quarters, 1 dime and 2 pennies. We can write this as 75 + 10 + 2 = ____ .
15. 32¢. There are 2 ones, 1 five and 1 twenty-five. We can write this as 2 + 5 + 25 = ____ .

3.4.A. Represent Data

1. 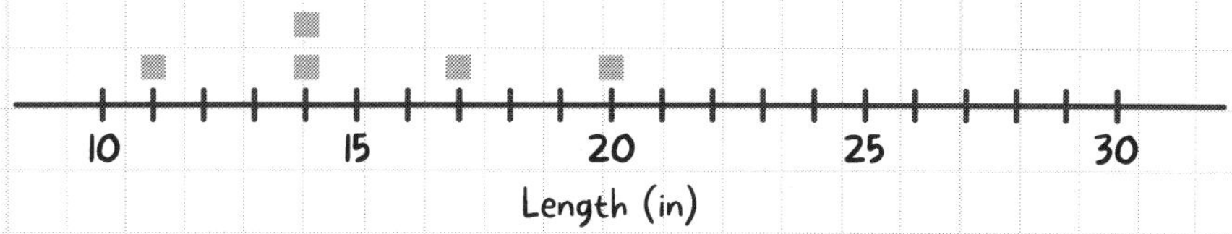

2. 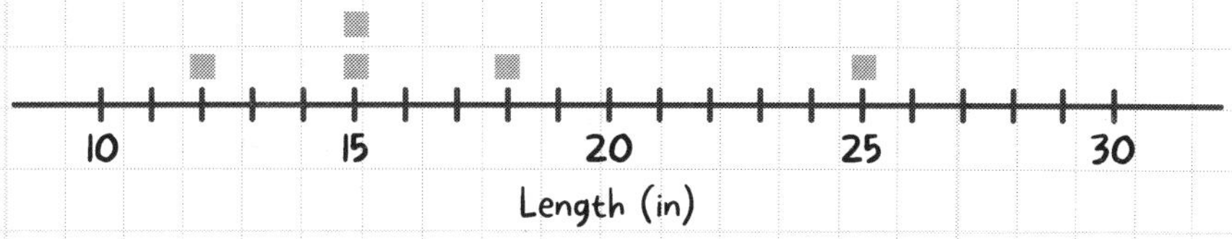

ANSWER SHEET

3.
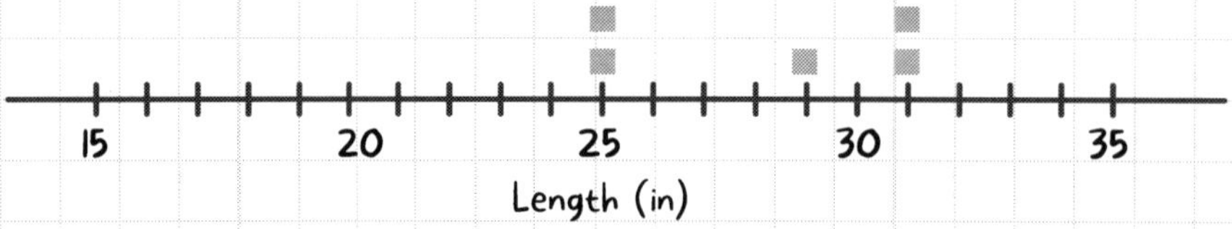

4.
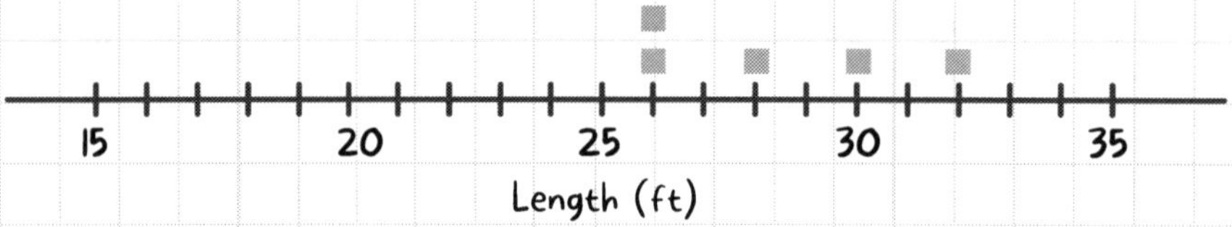

5.
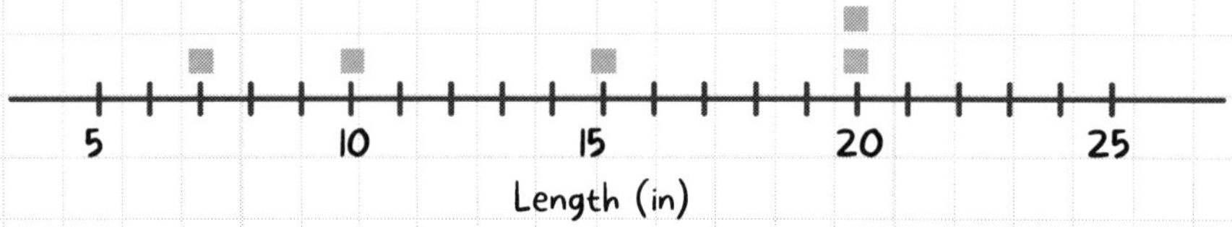

6.
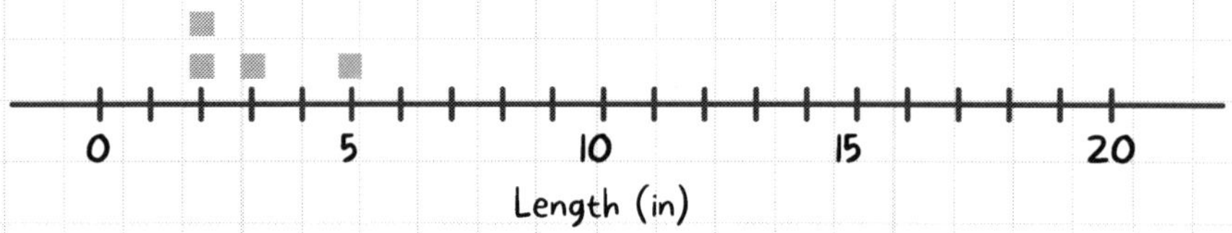

7.
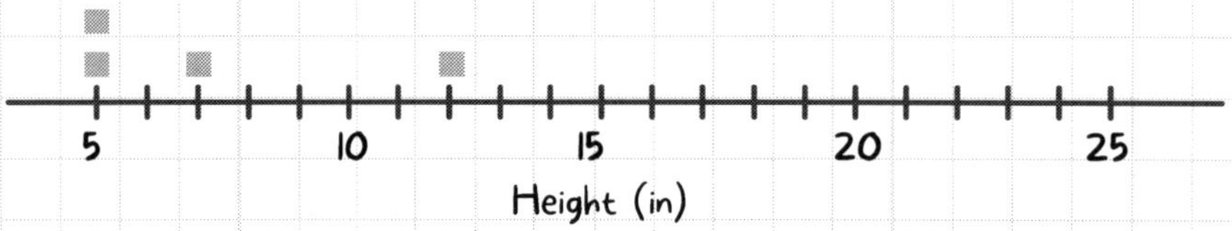

8.
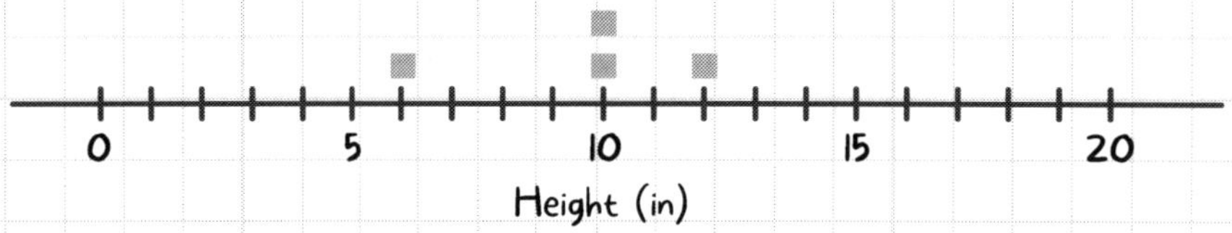

9.
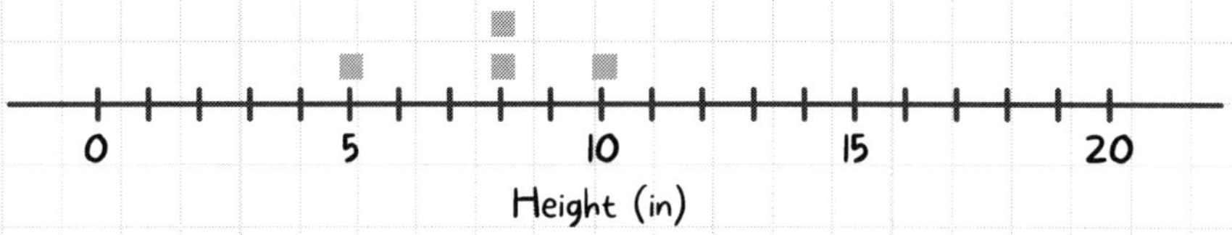

10.
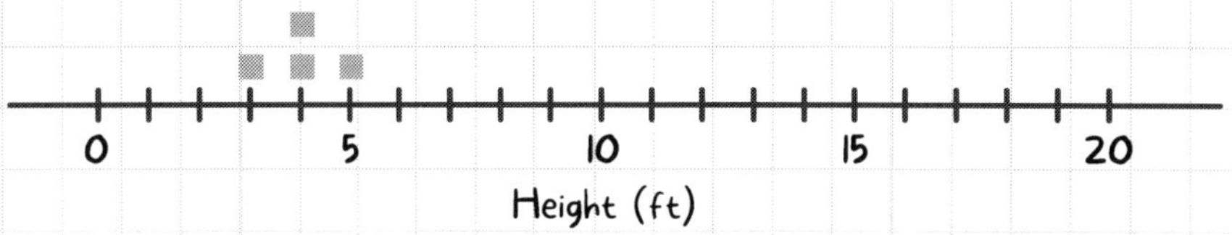

ANSWER SHEET

11. C. 5 ft appears in the data set three times.
12. B. 6 ft appears in the data set 2 times.
13. A. 9 ft appears in the data set 1 time.
14. A. 10 ft appears in the data set 1 time.

15.

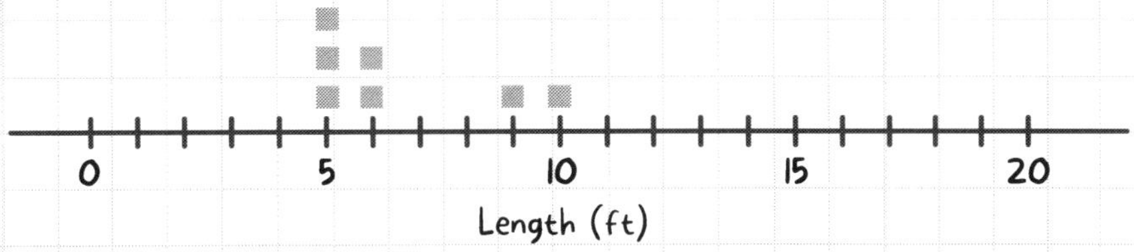

3.4.B. Interpret Data

1. B. Purple had 12 votes. Blue had 7 votes.
2. B. Purple has 12 votes. We can see that no other color received more votes because the bar for purple is the tallest.
3. C. Green had 3 votes. We can see that no other color received fewer votes because the bar for green is the shortest.
4. 16. 4 students voted for pink. 12 students voted for purple.
   The equation is 4 + 12.
5. 9. 12 students voted for purple. 3 students voted for green.
   The equation is 12 + 3.
6. Match the number of votes to the flavor of ice cream.

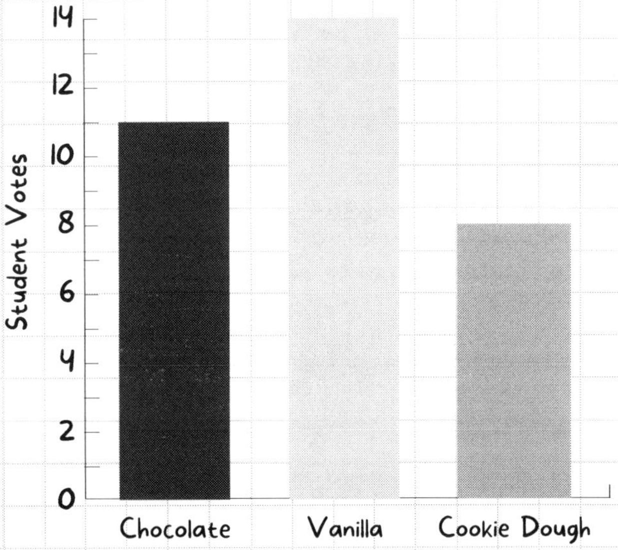

ANSWER SHEET

7. B. Vanilla has 14 votes. We can see that no other flavor received more votes because the bar for vanilla is the tallest.
8. C. Cookie dough had 8 votes. We can see that no other flavor received fewer votes because the bar for cookie dough is the shortest.
9. 25. Chocolate had 11 votes. Vanilla had 14 votes. The equation is 11 + 14
10. 3. Chocolate had 11 votes. Vanilla had 14 votes. The equation is 14 - 11
11. Draw the slices of pizza for person.

12. B. Betty ate 5 pieces of pizza. We can see that no other student ate more pizza because the picture row for Betty is the tallest.
13. C. Chris ate 1 piece of pizza. We can see that no other student ate less pizza because the picture row for Chris is the shortest.
14. 4. Betty ate 5 pieces of pizza. Christ ate 1 piece of pizza. The equation is 5 - 1.
15. 9. Add all of the data sets together. The equation is 3 + 5 + 1.

ANSWER SHEET

3.5. Chapter Test

1. 3 cm. Line the edge of the caterpillar up with zero hashmark on the centimeter side of the ruler.
2. 5 cm. Line the bottom of the caterpillar up with zero hashmark on the centimeter side of the ruler.
3. 2 in. Line the bottom of the caterpillar up with zero hashmark on the inch side of the ruler.
4. 1 in. Line the bottom of the caterpillar up with zero hashmark on the inch side of the ruler.
5. 15 ft. There are 3 ft in each yard. Since there are 5 ft in this problem, our equation is 3 + 3 + 3 + 3 + 3 = ____ , which equals 15.
6. 36 in. There are 12 inches in each foot. Since there are 3 feet, we can write the equation 12 + 12 + 12 = ____ , which equals 36.
7. 38 cm. This is an addition problem. The equation is 12 + 26 = ____ .
8. 27 students. This is a subtraction problem. The equation is 32 - 3 - 2 = ____ . Use a number line to hop backward 5 spaces.
9. B. This is an addition problem so the numbers will increase. Start at 11. Move forward 2 hashmarks for the adults, 3 for the toddlers and 1 for the babies.
10. The hour hand should be between the 5 and 6. The minute hand should be on the 3 (5 .... 10 .... 15).

11. 9:35. The hour hand is between the 9 and 10. The minute hand is on the 7 (5 .... 10 .... 15 .... 20 .... 25 .... 30 .... 35).
12. $40. There are 5 ones, 1 five and 3 tens. We can write this as 5 + 5 + 30 = ____ .
13. Answers may vary. Possible answers include 3 quarters; 7 dimes and 1 nickel; or 14 nickels .

ANSWER SHEET

14. 2 cm. The 1 cm mark is about half the height of the flower.
15. 1 inch. Line A is 2 inches long. Line B is 1 inch long. 2 - 1 = 1.
16. Plot each data point on the number line.

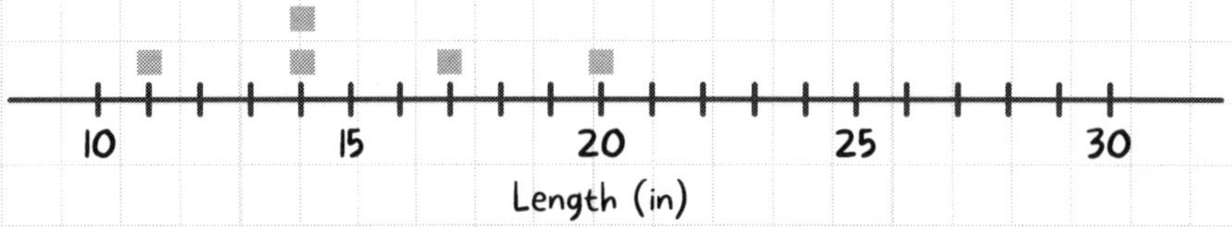

17. Plot each data point on the number line.

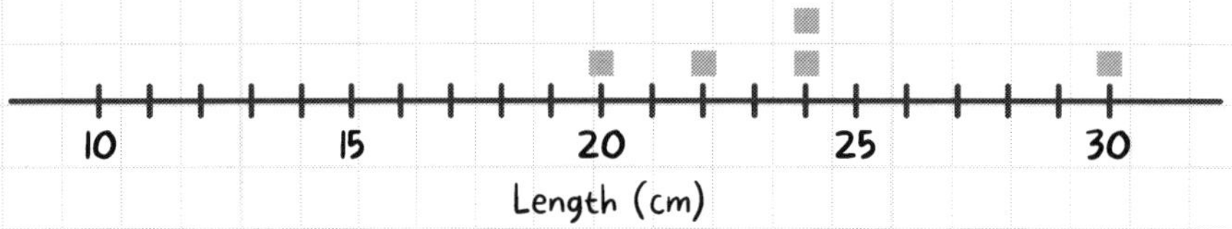

18.

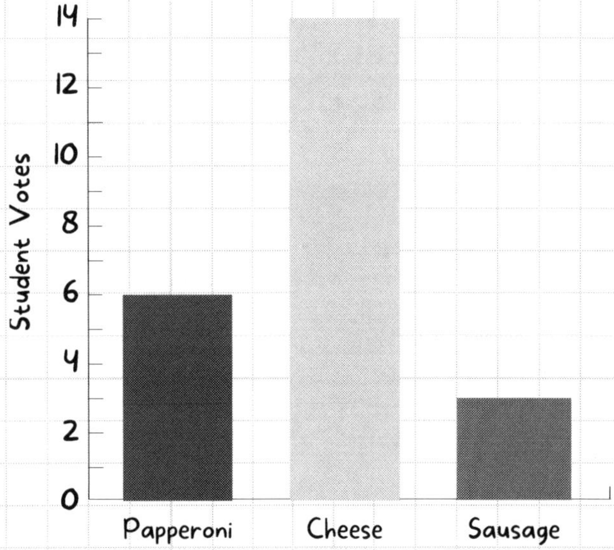

19. Cheese. Cheese received 14 votes. It also has the tallest bar.
20. Sausage. Sausage recevied 3 votes. It also has the shortest bar.

ANSWER SHEET

Chapter 4: Geometry

4.1.A. Recognizing and Drawing Shapes

1. Quadrilateral. Drawings may vary but should represent a closed shape with 4 straight sides.
2. Hexagon. Drawings may vary but should represent a closed shape with 6 straight sides.
3. Triangle. Drawings may vary but should represent a closed shape with 3 straight sides and 3 angles.
4. Pentagon. Drawings may vary but should represent a closed shape with 5 straight sides.
5. A, B, C. The fourth shape has is a closed shape but has 6 sides.
6. A, B, D. The third shape has three sides but is not a closed shape.
7. B, C, D. The first shape has more than 4 sides.
8. A, B. The third shape is a cube. The fourth shape is a pentagon.
9. Pentagon. A pentagon has 5 straight sides.
10. Quadrilateral. A quadrilateral has 4 straight sides.
11. Hexagon. A hexagon has 6 straight sides.
12. Answers may vary but should represent a closed shape with 4 straight sides.
13. Answers may vary but should represent a closed shape with 3 straight sides and 3 angles.
14. Answers may vary but should represent a closed shape with 5 straight sides.
15. Answers may vary but should represent a closed shape with 6 straight sides.

ANSWER SHEET

4.1.B. Partitioning Rectangles

1. 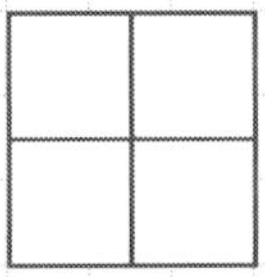
2. 4. There are 4 squares within the rectangle.
3. 2. Columns run up and down.
4. 2. Rows run side to side.
5. 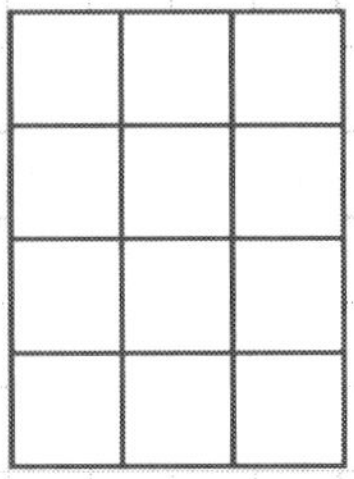
6. 12. There are 12 squares within the rectangle.
7. 4. There are 4 squares in each column.
8. 3. There are 3 squares in each row.
9. 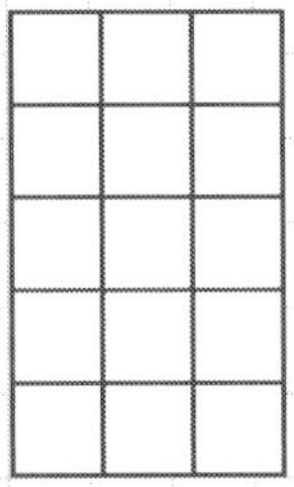
10. 15. There are 15 squares within the rectangle.
11. 5. There are 5 squares in each column.
12. 3. There are 3 squares in each row.
13. 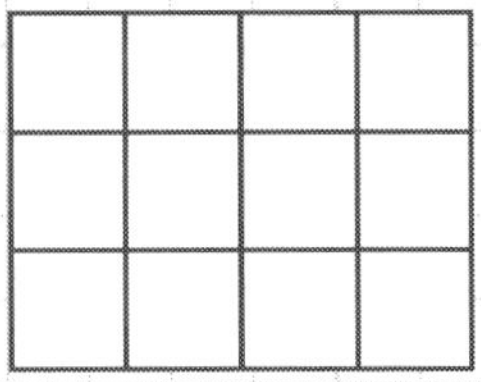
14. 12. There are 12 squares within the rectangle.
15. 3. There are 3 squares in each column.
16. 4. There are 4 squares in each row.

ANSWER SHEET

4.1.C. Partitioning Shapes into Halves, Thirds, and Fourths

1. B. The rectangle is divided into three equal parts.
2. C. The rectangle is divided into four equal parts.
3. A. The rectangle is divided into two equal parts.
4. B. The circle is divided into three equal parts.
5. A. The circle is divided into four equal parts.
6. C. The circle is divided into two equal parts.
7. Drawings may vary. Both rectangles should be divided into 2 equal parts.
8. Drawings may vary. Both rectangles should be divided into 3 equal parts.
9. Drawings may vary. Both rectangles should be divided into 4 equal parts.
10. A. The circle is divided into two equal parts.
11. C. The circle is divided into four equal parts.
12. B. The circle is divided into three equal parts.
13. B. Two out of two is one whole.
14. A. Three out of three is one whole.
15. C. Four out of four is one whole.

4.2. Chapter Test

1. A triangle is a closed shape with 3 sides and 3 angles.
2. A pentagon is a closed shape with 5 straight sides.
3. A hexagon is a closed shape with 6 straight sides.
4. A quadrilateral is a closed shape with 4 straight sides.
5. A, B, C. The fourth shape has 6 sides instead of 5 sides.
6. A, B, D. The third shape has more than 6 sides.
7. Answers may vary but should represent a closed shape with 4 straight sides.
8. Hexagon. A hexagon has 6 straight sides.
9. 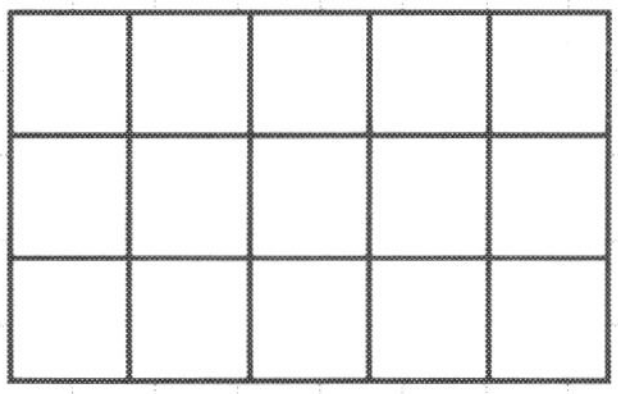

ANSWER SHEET

10. 15 squares. There are 15 squares in all.
11. 5 squares. There are 5 squares in each row.
12. 3 squares. There are 3 squares in each column.
13. The circle is partitioned into two equal parts.

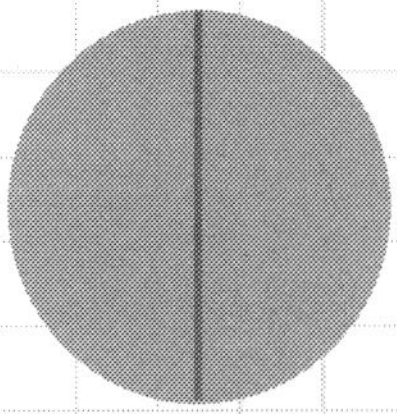

or

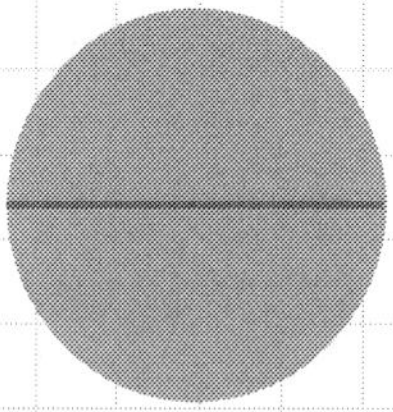

14. The circle is partitioned into three equal parts.

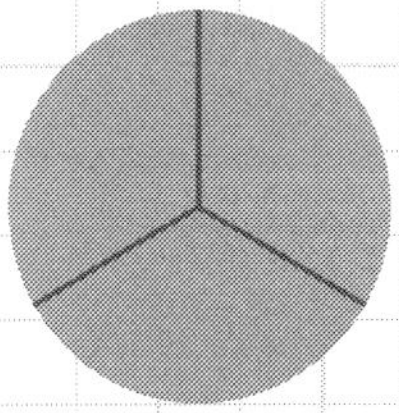

15. The circle is partitioned into four equal parts.

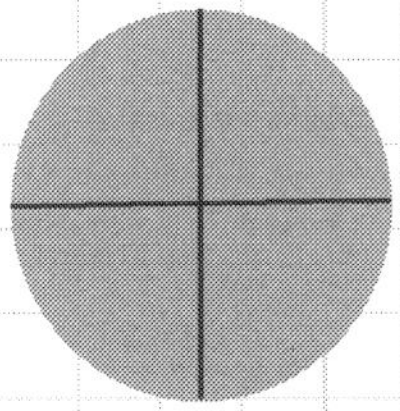

16. Two rows across. Two columns up and down.

17. 4 squares. There are 4 squares in all.
18. 2. There are 2 squares in each row.
19. 2. There are 2 squares in each column.
20. C. Each square represents one out of four squares, which is one-fourth.

ARGOPREP

ANSWER SHEET

Chapter 5: Mixed Assessment

1. 71. This is an addition problem. The equation is 45 + 26.
2. 60. This is an addition problem. The equation is 35 + 25.
3. 13. This is a two-step problem. First subtract 6 from 14, then add 5 to the difference.
4. 47. This is an addition problem. The equation is 32 + 15.
5. 43. 52 + ____ = 95 Subtract 52 from 95 to find the missing addend.
6. 9. Use number relationships or make an easier problem.
7. 9. Use number relationships or make an easier problem.
8. 6. Use number relationships or make an easier problem.
9. 4. Use number relationships or make an easier problem.
10. 22. Count on or decompose.
11. 24. Count on or decompose.
12. 107. Count on or decompose.
13. 21. Count on or decompose.
14. No. It can't be split into two equal groups.
15. Yes. It can be split into two equal groups of 8.
16. Yes. They can be split into two equal groups of 3.
17. No. They can't be split into two equal groups.
18. 3 + 3 + 3. 3 rows of 3.
19. 4 + 4. 2 rows of 4.
20. 5 + 5 + 5. 3 rows of 5.
21. 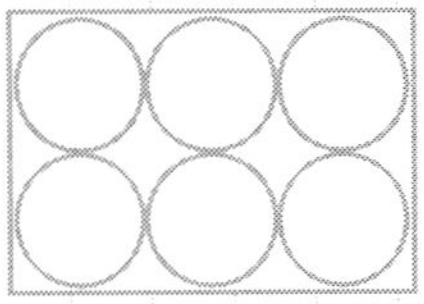
22. 6. 3 + 3 = 6.
23. 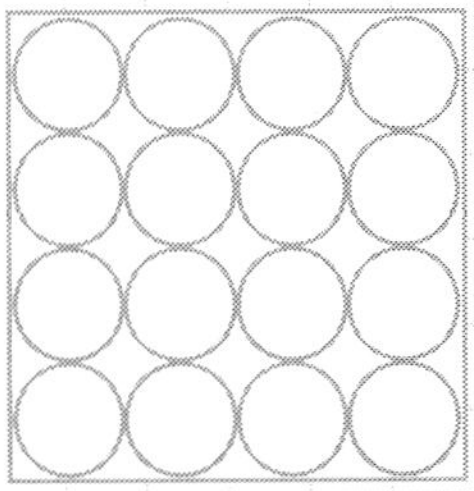

ANSWER SHEET

24. 16. 4 + 4 + 4 + 4 = 16.
25. 150, 250, 350, 450. The hundreds digit increases by 1 each time
26. 150, 160, 170, 180. The tens digit increases by 1 each time.
27. 150, 155, 160, 165. The ones digit increases by 5 each time.
28. 48 tens 7 ones. 10 tens equals 100. 40 tens equals 400, 8 tens equals 80 and 7 ones equals 7.
29. 291. 200 + 90 + 1.
30. 536. 400 + 100 + 30 + 6.
31. C. 5 hundreds, 3 tens, 4 ones.
32. B. 621 is ten more than 612. The tens digit is greater by one digit.
33. C. The numbers are equal.
34. B. 307 is greater than 37.
35. 7, 47, 407, 470. Use place value to order the numbers.
36. 217, 271, 712, 721. Use place value to order the numbers.
37. 412. The hundreds digit decreases by one.
38. 812. The hundreds digit decreases by one.
39. 369. The tens digit increases by 2.
40. 623. The tens digit decreases by 6.
41. 89.
42. 135. First add 30 and 10. Then add 52 and 43. Combine the sums to get 135 .
43. 181. First add 45 and 55. Then add the sum to 65. Break 16 up into 10 and 6 and add it to the result.
44. 612. Explanations may vary but should demonstrate knowledge of place value or operations.
45. 202. Explanations may vary but should demonstrate knowledge of place value or operations.
46. 167. This is a multistep addition problem. The equation is 76 + 27 + 64.
47. 46. The equation is 63 - 17.
48. 9cm. Use the ruler to find the measurement.
49. 5cm. Use the ruler to find the measurement.
50. 5 in. Use the ruler to find the measurement.
51. 2 in. Use the ruler to find the measurement.
52. Line A is 1 inch longer than Line B.

ANSWER SHEET

53. 21 ft. 3 + 3 + 3 + 3 + 3 +3 + 3.
54. 72 in. 12 + 12 + 12 + 12 + 12 + 12.
55. 2 ft. It takes 2 feet to make 24 inches.
56. 5. There are 100 cm in each meter.
57. 98. Add 52 to 46.
58. 22. Start at 33. Hop back 7. Then hop back 4 (you can also hop back 10 and then hop back 1).
59. 16. Start at 11. Then hop forward 2. Hop forward 3 more.
60. 45. 5 ones, 2 fives, 3 tens is the same as 5 + 5 + 5 + 10 + 10 + 10.
61. Answers may vary. Possible answers include 1 quarter and 1 dime or 3 dimes and 1 nickel.
62. Answers may vary. Possible answers include 3 quarters, 1 nickel and 1 penny or 8 dimes and 1 penny.
63. 71 ¢. 25 + 25 + 10 + 5 + 5 + 1.
64. 39 ¢. 10 + 10 + 10 + 5 + 4.
65. The big hand is on the 5. The small hand is on the 7.
66. The big hand is on the 2. The small hand is on the 11.
67. 5:45.
68. 2:55.
69. There should be 3 dots above the 14, 1 dot above the 18 and 1 dot above the 21.
70. There should be 1 dot above the 15, 1 dot above the 18, 2 dots above the 21 and 2 dots above the 27.
71.

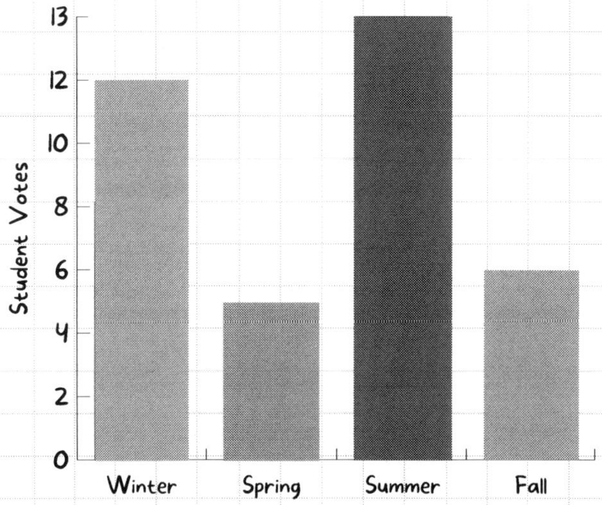

ANSWER SHEET

72. Summer. It has the tallest bar on the graph.
73. Spring. It has the shortest bar on the graph.

74.

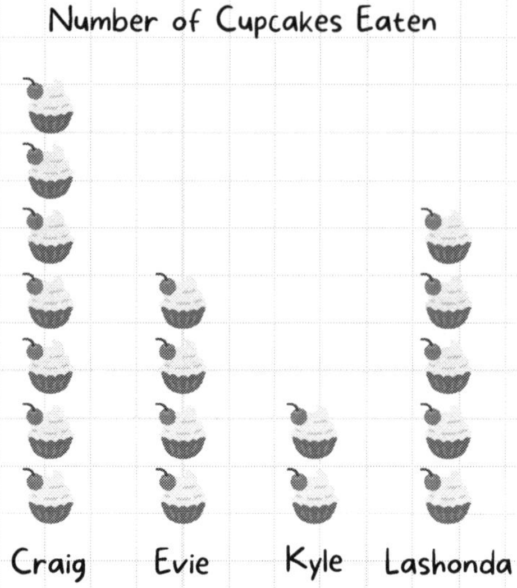

75. Craig. He has the most cupcakes by his name.
76. Kyle. He has the fewest cupcakes by his name.
77. 5. Craig has 5 more cupcakes than Kyle on the chart.
78. 18. There are 18 total cupcakes on the chart.
79. Pentagon. Drawings may vary, but should have 5 sides.
80. Triangle. Drawings may vary, but should have 3 sides and 3 angles.

81.

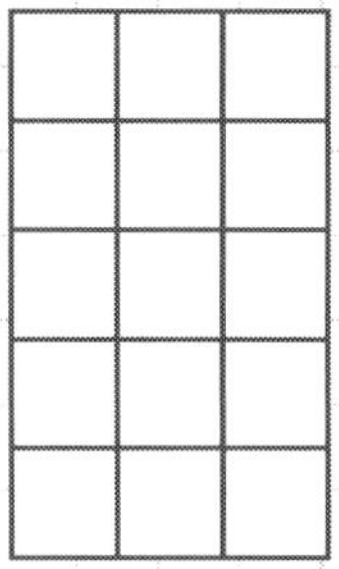

82. 15. There are 15 total squares. 5 + 5 + 5.
83. 3. There are 3 squares across each row.
84. 5. There are 5 squares down each column.

ANSWER SHEET

85. 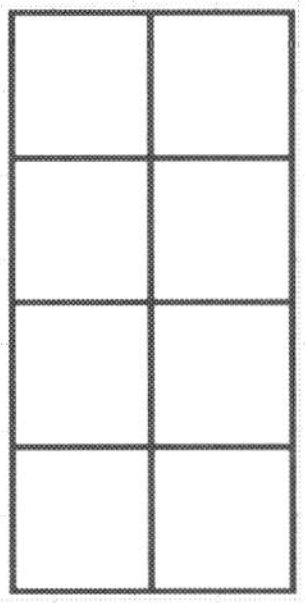

86. 8. There are 8 total boxes. Count each one or use the equation 2 + 2+ 2 + 2.

87. 2. There are 2 squares across each row.

88. 4. There are 4 squares down each column.

89. 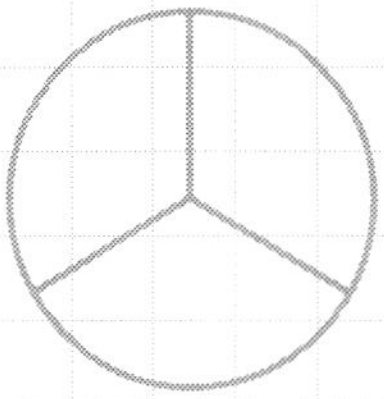

90. B. There are three sections.

91. 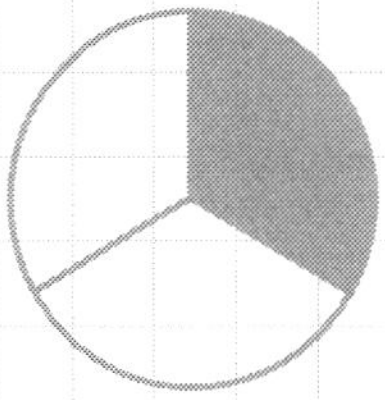

92. 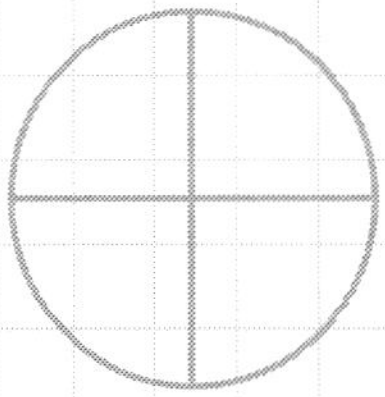

93. C. There are 4 sections.

94. 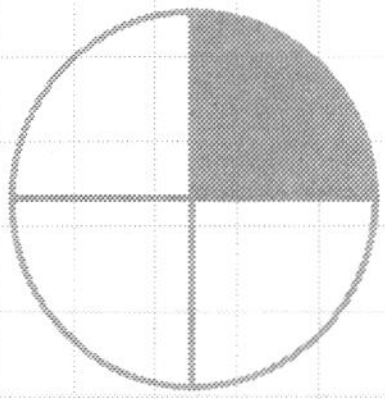

ANSWER SHEET

95. 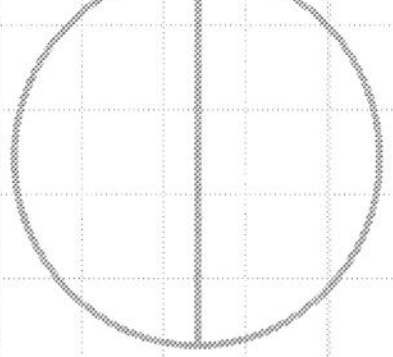

96. A. There are 2 sections.

97. 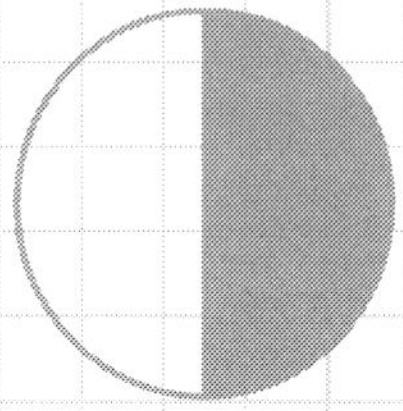

98. A and C. The other shapes have more than 3 sides.
99. A, C and D. The other shapes have more than 5 sides.
100. B and C. The other shapes have more or less than 6 sides.

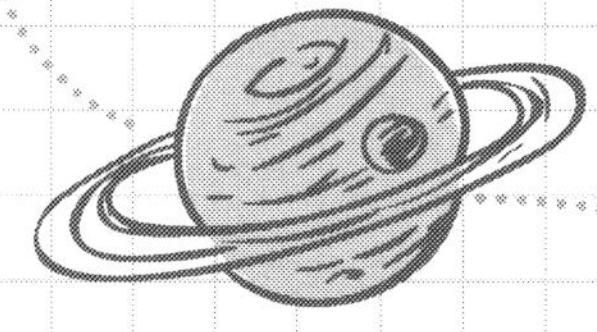

Made in the USA
Middletown, DE
30 September 2020

20872550R00163